STACI BOYER

MEDALLION
P R E S S

Medallion Press, Inc.
medallionpress.com

Published 2010 by Medallion Press, Inc.

The MEDALLION PRESS LOGO
is a registered trademark of Medallion Press, Inc.

Manuscript prepared by Melissa Killian, Killian Creative, Boulder, Colorado.
www.killiancreative.com

Typeset in Adobe Garamond Pro
Printed in the United States of America

ISBN: 978-1-605420-92-9

10 9 8 7 6 5 4 3 2 1

First Edition

DEDICATION

This book is dedicated to my father, Cliff Frank Drown, and Grandmother Lawana Drown Berg. Sadly, both have passed, but their memories and the person they helped me to become are alive in this book forever!

CONTENTS

FOREWORD

The ancient root of the word *enthusiasm* is *entheos*, meaning literally *the fire of the gods*. The word is *fire*. Not *charisma* or *charm*, which are both too easy, and in the end, alone, are empty of substance. I write of a motivated and motivating fire, which, if possessed by the right teacher, can create an inspired vision with goals attainable by anyone, at any age, anywhere. Sadly, it is a fire many fitness and wellness professionals seem to have long ago surrendered to a host of gimmicks and fads, resulting in nothing but frustration and lost hope.

Twelve years ago, I was teaching a sports science class in Chicago—a session I thought would be cancelled due to an unexpected blizzard. That morning, I encountered fire personified in the first student to arrive, the remarkable Staci Boyer.

Through the years, I have been privileged to witness this inspired flame grow and touch the lives of countless others. As a mother of two wonderful boys and a wife. As a community leader organizing seemingly endless programs to help those less fortunate. As a truly inspiring motivational speaker who delivers both education and inspiration to groups across the nation. As a multi-award-winning certified personal trainer, two-time master trainer, author, and wellness coach.

Staci Boyer is the epitome of motivation and inspiration. Her energy is boundless and, through her life's work, has the effect of lighting up those around her. When you meet her, you sense immediately the depth to which this inspired vision runs. It is something that, in another age, might have been labeled a *magnificent obsession*.

Staci has dedicated herself to help anyone at any age experience a truly motivated and healthy life. She has proven it through her lectures and classes across the country. I've witnessed on many occasions the ovations she has received after presentations which brought the seemingly impossible within grasp.

Through her groundbreaking work, *Motiv8n' U*, you will have the opportunity to meet this remarkable woman, grow from the knowledge she shares, and experience that motivating fire, which is both warming and inspiring. But as you follow her life's journey, you will soon realize this fire is forged in the furnace of achievement *and* affliction. Her path has not been an easy one, by any means. And yet, despite the challenges she has encountered, which would have caused many to quit, she has chosen to grow and teach others how to move beyond their obstacles to experience a fulfilling life.

Through my own journey as a doctor, teacher, master trainer, and consultant, I have witnessed the remarkable achievements of the professional and Olympic champions I have served. But are these accomplishments solely the rights of those born on Mt. Olympus, with the appropriate genetics and opportunities? To many real people, the ability to create lasting change seems out of reach, both physically and emotionally. But through *Motiv8n' U,* Staci Boyer applies her vast experience to proven techniques to provide a path out of frustration and into the experience of a fit, strong body and spirit carrying readers toward their dreams.

In these pages, Staci has mapped out an innovative two-part plan to help you achieve a healthy and truly enthusiastic life.

Part One will motivate you to start on this path and maintain the momentum once you begin. The CORE foundational concepts immediately demonstrate that Staci, as your coach, respects both you and your goals and is truly walking by your side along this exciting path.

Part Two continues the journey by presenting eight powerful principles of change that will help you arrive at your goals. These principles can be applied by anyone, of any age, to reach any goal. They concern your inner well-being as well as your outer transformation in strength and fulfillment.

In over twenty-five years of working with some of the world's greatest athletes and performing artists, I have seen it all. Through Staci Boyer and her tireless dedication, I have experienced what every teacher truly dreams of: a student who has taken everything offered and found every possible way to share her knowledge, inspiration, motivation, and that sacred fire with everyone she meets.

I once spoke with Staci about her time serving our country in the United States Navy during the Persian Gulf War. She told me about a time when, while she served as a hospital corpsman on the Navy hospital ship *Comfort*, warning sirens signaled imminent attack. I asked, "What did you do?" I could have guessed the reply: "I just did my duty. I took care of people who needed my help and tried to make a difference."

This is one example of Staci's commitment to those she serves, and this is the kind of support and dedication you will be surprised to feel coming through the pages of *Motiv8n' U*.

I am always proud to introduce Staci Boyer to all I know and am equally honored to introduce *you* to this motivating leader. As you experience the enthusiastic fire found within the pages of *Motiv8n' U,* I know your life goals for health and wellness will be ignited and soon become a beacon for many others in the years to come.

Dr. Jack Barnathan

President, N.Y. Strength Inc.

Strength is defined not by the
absence of moments of weakness

but by our ability to
overcome in those
moments.

★ ★ INTRODUCTION ★ ★

BEEN THERE, DONE THAT!

> You gain strength, courage and confidence by every experience in which you really stop to look fear in the face. You are able to say to yourself, "I lived through this. . . . I can take the next thing that comes along."
>
> You must do the thing you think you cannot do.
>
> Eleanor Roosevelt

Have you ever stopped to wonder what happened to the dreams you had for yourself— dreams of exciting work, a happy family life, looking great, and actually making a difference in the world? I have.

Wherever you are in life right now, chances are I've been there. Whether you're at the top or the bottom of the mountain, at home or homeless, in shape or out, I've been there.

I'm here to tell you, if I can climb out of some of the deepest pits, bounce back from the most deflating setbacks, and make the most of the worst circumstances, so can you. I promise you, there is no situation you can't overcome if you set your mind to it.

Overweight? Out of shape? Jobless? Homeless? I've been there. Despairing over your marriage, finances, a bankruptcy, or foreclosure? You're not alone. Maybe you're simply stuck in the funk of everyday living, feeling restless, bored, and discontented. Hey, I've been there, too.

I've been down many dead-end streets that forced me to face these very same issues, but in the process I found ways to turn things around and get back on the right road again. In fact, turning your life around is not as complicated as you might think. Your life can be maneuvered through some fairly narrow passageways and turn on a dime.

This is how quickly things can turn around for you: In a week, you can radically change how you feel. In a month, you can radically change how you look.

I don't care if you are eighteen or eighty. I have helped men and women of all ages point their lives in the direction of their dreams. Whether you're a young lady preparing to participate in the Miss America pageant, a soccer mom wondering what happened to your figure, or a retiree looking to make a difference in the lives of others, the principles and processes are the same. You just need thirty quality days to swab the deck, repair the sails, and get the ship of your life back on course.

Experts say it takes thirty days to form a habit. That's not very long in the grand scheme of things. If you're a mom, a college student, a new employee, or an empty nester wondering what to do with your life now, I am telling you that if you will give me thirty days, together we can begin to change your present and future reality. Sure, it might take longer to drop all of the weight you'd like or to redirect your life so it's more fulfilling, but all of that will come with replacing bad habits with good ones. In thirty days, you can establish lifelong fitness habits that will rock your entire world!

Renowned business philosopher Jim Rohn once said, "Motivation is what gets you started. Habit is what keeps you going." Once you discover what truly motivates you, you can begin putting the habits into place to reshape yourself—and your future. In eight days, you will see a difference; in eight weeks everyone around you will see a difference; in eight months you will have accomplished more than you have in the last eight years; and by the end of the next decade, you'll have done more than you ever thought possible. There is no limit to what you can accomplish if you simply form the habits that will get you there.

I know this probably sounds too good to be true considering how busy you are. I understand! I am married and have two children—Corbin, twelve, and Drew, five. I run my own business as a personal fitness trainer, motivational speaker, and consultant, which requires quite a bit of traveling. I am also the official trainer for the Miss Illinois Scholarship Association, am working toward my master's degree in social work, and within the last three years have competed in three fitness competitions—Bikini

Universe, Mid-Illinois Bodybuilding and Figure Championship, and Fitness America Pageant Midwest—placing first runner-up in all. (Check me out in the finals on my Web site at www.staciboyer.com.) Believe me: I know what busy is!

So is it too much to expect to have a successful career, a vibrant marriage, a well-tended family, a tidy house, and a tight behind? Not if you form the right habits.

No, you can't do everything, but if you do the *right* things, it's surprising how much of the rest will take care of itself.

And there's more good news. The keys you need to succeed are already inside of you. We just need to bring them out into the open and let them begin unlocking your best future. By doing the right things—simply making the right choices—you can build the foundational strength you need in *all* areas of your life to see you through any challenge. I am not saying it's easy—just that it's possible and so, so worth it!

This book is about getting not only your body but your life in shape. That means starting your day off right by choosing to be your best self; maintaining your kitchen so you and your family can eat right every day; organizing your closet and your checkbook so you, not your stuff or your money, control your life; and dreaming big about the legacy you leave. Being healthy is not just about fitting into your skinny jeans. It's about sleeping through the night; being productive at work; having energy to play with your children; following your dreams; and, of course, having the spunk to find your way to the squat rack.

Fitness is an overall state of health and wellness. It's a puzzle we need all of the pieces to complete. When we have quality in the eight areas of whole-life fitness, we make a quality life. As you will see in the pages ahead, those eight areas are financial, organizational, relational, vocational, emotional, spiritual, nutritional, and "funny bone" fitness.

And it all starts with the first thirty days, the time you'll need to thoroughly integrate the principles and practices that will get you where you want to go from here on out.

To that end, I have organized this book into two parts addressing the two main areas you'll need to master to get fit and stay fit in all areas of your life.

Part One is about finding the motivation necessary to start on the right path and keep going even when you want to quit. The four chapters in Part One highlight four CORE concepts: choices, ownership, refining vision and taking responsibility, and engagement. You'll discover what core issues drive you, how to read your inner compass, and how you can draw strength from past experiences to propel you forward.

Part Two presents the eight core tips that will take you from where you are now to where you want to be. These action steps spell out the word STRENGTH and include setting SMART goals,[1] thinking about what you want, revving up your relationships, empowering yourself, negating the negatives, giving back with gratitude, taking charge, and harnessing the power of honesty, humility, and humor.

Together, these concepts and action steps work to form the CORE STRENGTH we all need to lead lives worth living and chase the dreams we all so deeply desire.

Along the way, I've included space for you to answer some important questions that will help you gauge where you are in your personal journey to CORE STRENGTH. Are you ready to get started? Great! Then turn the page. You've got some new choices to make to get you up and running!

> You cannot change your destination overnight, but you can change your direction overnight.
>
> Jim Rohn

---

1. Doran, George T. "There's a S.M.A.R.T. Way to Write Management Goals and Objectives, *Management Review* 70.11, November 1981.

Motivation (mō'te-vā'shen): the psychological feature that arouses an organism to action toward a desired goal; the reason for the action; that which gives purpose and direction to behavior.[2]

What's Motiv8n' U?

2. *WordNet: A Lexical Database for English*, s.v. "motivation," http://wordnetweb.princeton.edu/perl/webwn?s=motivation (accessed February 2, 2009).

PART ONE

ESTABLISHING A STRONG CORE

**EVERY MOVEMENT YOU MAKE BEGINS FROM
YOUR CENTER OF POWER.**

THE FOUR ESSENTIAL ELEMENTS OF A STRONG CORE

> If you want to make your dreams come true,
> the first thing you have to do is wake up.

J.M. Power

Who are you, really, and what do you really want? When do you feel the most alive? What genuinely motivates *you*?

I want you to wake up to what really motivates you, to identify and draw strength from those things that inspire and stimulate you, and to understand what deflates and de-energizes you.

The four chapters of this first section will help you establish your true inner motives. They are like the four legs of a table. Without each one firmly in place and balanced, the table won't stand, or at least it won't bear any weight. I want to help you build a sturdy table that will hold all of the settings and centerpieces you want to put on display, a strong table that's not lopsided or wobbly and won't collapse when someone leans on it. We're talking about CORE STRENGTH, inner strength unseen at first glance.

True strength, or CORE STRENGTH, works from the inside out. Not just beginning with your gut muscles but from your innermost thoughts, beliefs, and values. It is a strength pervading every area of your life so everything works together congruously: a systemic, holistic, comprehensive strength encompassing every aspect of your being. In other words, functional fitness, or fitness with a purpose, is about more than toning your muscles; it's about toning your mind. It's a mind-set that translates into a lifestyle.

True fitness is strength of character to overcome obstacles, bear heavy burdens, endure tough situations, and persevere in believing and doing the very best. It's about flexibility, balance, control, and poise under pressure. When you are mentally and physically fit, you have an inner peace and a sense of freedom in knowing you are the master of your mind and your body, and that mastery extends into your ability to command your reality, your potential, and even your destiny.

In 1902, James Allen wrote the revolutionary *As a Man Thinketh*, in which he stated, "The outer conditions of a person's life will always be found to reflect their inner beliefs," and "All that a man achieves and all that he fails to achieve is the direct result of his own thoughts." I also like what Golda Meir once said: "Trust yourself. Create the kind of self that you will be happy to live with all your life. Make the most of yourself by fanning the tiny, inner sparks of possibility into flames of achievement." As you read on, I want you to take a good look at the kind of self you will be happy to live with for the rest of your life.

Getting motivated begins with understanding what motivates *you*. It involves some self-reflection and understanding of your inner drives and desires, as well as your inner demons and destructive thought patterns. Most of us don't even realize the behaviors and habits sabotaging our best efforts to change. Some of us don't even realize we need to change.

A Russian philosopher named George Gurdjieff concluded, "Self-observation brings man to the realization of the necessity of self-change." This observation, he wrote, is the catalyst for change: "And in observing himself a man notices that self-observation itself brings about certain changes in his inner processes. He begins to understand that self-observation is an instrument of self-change, a means of awakening." As Allen did, Gurdjieff believed that what you produce in your mind is ultimately what you produce in your life, and the best life you could produce begins with self-knowledge.

The outer you is a result of the inner you, so let's get started producing your best life from the inside out.

Fitness is the result of developing your heart and soul muscles as much as your abdominal muscles. Motivation begins in the heart, with an inner desire. It begins with a mind-set of core beliefs and motives. In the next four chapters, you will explore the source of those motives, harness and build upon them, and generate the momentum to stay motivated to maximize your strength, fitness, and *freedom* in every area of life. Let's get started producing your best life from the inside out.

> They themselves are makers of themselves by virtue of the thoughts which they choose and encourage; that mind is the master weaver, both of the inner garment of character and the outer garment of circumstance, and that, as they may have hitherto woven in ignorance and pain they may now weave in enlightenment and happiness.
>
> James Allen

Your destiny is not by chance—

it is by choice.

CHOOSE TO MAKE A CHANGE

CHAPTER 1

Life is a sum of all your choices.

Albert Camus

As an eight-year-old, I was one of the smallest in my class. So when my father offered to sponsor a basketball team through his work (he even let me name it The Mermaids), my first reaction sounded something like this: "How can I be any good at basketball? I am too short. I can't jump. I don't even know how to play."

This soon turned into a life-defining moment. My father's response opened my eyes to the power I had to choose my destiny. He said, "Staci, you can run faster than any of them. Basketball is not just about height; it's also about speed. If you choose to own what you're good at, it's yours." From that moment on, I did own it. I became a point guard who would be wherever the ball was and move to the basket at least a step ahead of everyone else.

My dad's words have stuck with me ever since. They haven't kept me from making some mistakes along the way, but they have made all the difference in helping me turn those mistakes around. I can still hear him saying, "Your destiny is not by chance—it is by choice. If you want to make me proud, then you will have to make the right choices and not let yourself be limited by what you *don't* have. You will have to do the best you can with what you *do* have." I have learned that life is one choice at a time, moving you closer or further away from your heart's truest desires.

So why don't our choices always line up with our desires? Why do we choose to do things that take us off course or completely derail our plans? In my life, I have made some bad choices and some good ones. I made the good ones when I had the courage to do what I knew was right; they were made from a place of strength, engaging my innermost convictions. I have found that when I have the courage to own the past, take responsibility for the present, and actively engage in a vision for the future I truly desire, my choices are healthy and productive. On the other hand, when I am off balance, when I can't see clearly because I am afraid, angry, confused, or simply in denial, my choices can be very unhealthy and destructive. I have been in some dark and desperate places that led me to make some bad decisions. But through those experiences, I have learned that anyone can choose to turn things around with a few simple steps.

> In the long run, we shape our lives, and we shape ourselves. The process never ends until we die. And the choices we make are ultimately our own responsibility.
>
> Eleanor Roosevelt

I WAS THE PROVERBIAL UGLY DUCKLING

Even though I had a great dad, my childhood was far from ideal. We moved constantly because of my father's work, and by the time I was in middle school, I had come to know three different mothers. Yet this was only the beginning. By the time I graduated from high school, I had also been kicked out of three different homes.

My transitory life began when I was born and given up for adoption because my natural mother was in no shape to keep me. My earliest memories are of Scotland, where my adoptive family moved when my father's company relocated him there. For kindergarten, I remember going to boarding school, the Albyn School for Girls, and only returning home on the weekends. My parents didn't live far away, but for some reason I lived in a boardinghouse with a nanny and other children from the school. I think my parents felt a little guilty, because I remember Santa coming twice that year with a ton of presents.

After my kindergarten year, we moved back to the U.S. to live in Louisiana. My father must have been making good money in those days, because I again attended a private school. But we weren't so wealthy that I could keep up with the designer styles the other kids wore.

Having the wrong clothes doesn't help a girl fit in, but I had more than my wardrobe working against me. I looked a lot like my twelve-year-old son does now. I mean, he is cute for a boy, but I was a girl. I recently showed my son a picture of myself at that age, and he asked me if people ever thought I was a boy. I had to admit, "Yeah, all the time."

Private school kids—I suppose all kids, really—can be rough on the ones who don't fit in. They were certainly tough on me, teasing and bullying. I felt as if I couldn't hold my head up—except, that is, when I was on the basketball court. But even that wasn't enough to make walking down the halls any easier.

There came a day in sixth grade when I made a choice. I had to take a stand or remain the doormat everyone else wiped their feet on. I remember the day I decided I wouldn't put up with any more. I walked onto the bus and heard the kids singing their songs and mocking me *again*. I endured the taunting all the way to my stop—but when it was time to exit, I determined I would never let them tease me again. There had to be something better for me out there. There were other people; there were other schools. So I made a choice. I got up, turned to the bus full of kids, told them in no uncertain terms where they could get off, and then ran off the bus and all the way home, where I informed my daddy I would never go back to that school again.

The next day, my dad enrolled me in public school, where I finished sixth grade.

This was a big change for me. I had made a choice. I had found my voice, spoken up, and started expecting more out of life right then and there as a little girl. I determined I wouldn't be the ugly duckling anymore.

But it wouldn't be easy.

One of the first big blows came before the end of the school year. I came home one day to find a big North Atlantic Moving Company van in the front yard. My mom, Carol, was moving out, and no one had said anything to me about it. She loaded all of her stuff up that day and left us.

I don't remember many of the details, but my dad did the best he could to put things back together, though he must have felt pretty lost and like running away himself. That summer he rented an RV and took my friend Allison and me out on the road to see the sights.

I know it might seem strange that I would end up with my dad instead of my mom, but for some reason I never really thought about it. Not long after Carol left, I would find out why.

The next year, I went to Webb Boarding School in Bell Buckle, Tennessee. It was a hard time for me because I missed my dad so much, but I also credit this year and this school for much of the creative teaching ability I have today. It was a great place with an incredibly amazing group of teachers. One of the things I remember from this year was learning to say the Greek alphabet before a paper match burned out. This was also a unique way of teaching us how to memorize formulas. The faculty really thought outside of the box!

Even though I liked this school, by Christmas I was so lonely I convinced my dad to let me come home. Before the year was out, I was back with him and—surprise!—his new wife, Peggy. By this time Dad was living near Houston, so I finished seventh grade and started eighth at Knox Junior High in Woodlands, Texas.

Around this time I began putting two and two together and figured out why I'd stayed with my dad after the divorce. I was looking through family photo albums with my grandmother and noticed I looked more like my grandmother's niece than anyone else in the family. After pressing the issue, I discovered that, sure enough, my dad's cousin was my birth mother. She was very young, irresponsible, and unmarried when she had me, so her cousin adopted me. It was strange to learn that another member of my dad's family was my real parent. When she suddenly died of a heart attack only a few years after I figured out who she really was, I was horrified.

I'd lost two mothers just as I was trying to establish my identity as an adolescent. This would have taken an emotional toll on any kid, but during this especially confusing time, I made the decision to move forward and be the most beautiful me I could be.

After the trauma of being the ugly duckling in grade school, I began to remake myself little by little. I let my hair grow longer and, sometime in middle school, started to wear more makeup and pay more attention to my appearance. Like a typical teenager, I overdid it a little, and at one point my dad temporarily confiscated my makeup. I learned it was important to look your best, but from my father I learned there is more to a person than her appearance. Dad taught me that if you don't have a beautiful heart inside, having long hair and thick eyelashes is really a waste. Beauty radiates from within.

I took some modeling classes at this time, which taught me how to carry myself with confidence and poise. I practiced runway modeling and actually got pretty good at it. This experience helped me develop stage presence and the ability to look audience members in the eyes. Looking back, I realize it probably helped me to become the confident speaker and presenter I am today, too.

Although I was an awkward, tomboyish tweener, by the end of ninth grade, I had the confidence to go out for cheerleading—and I made it. This really changed the way everyone, even I, saw me.

> Life is change. Growth is optional. Choose wisely.
>
> Author Unknown

OKAY, SO WHAT?

Why am I telling you all of this? Because I want you to see that no matter what life throws at you, you always have a choice. You can see your past either as an obstacle holding you back or a valuable lesson propelling you into a better future. I won't tell you the past doesn't matter, because I think it does. But life doesn't hand you excuses for not succeeding; it hands you lessons for improving yourself. Your past is what has shaped you into the person you are today. Celebrate your successes, and learn from your defeats. Dissect your mistakes, and choose to make a change. Throw the rotten things in the compost to fertilize the good things you are cultivating in yourself.

Remember: Your destiny is not by chance—it is by choice.

To figure out where you are going, you have to figure out where you are now; and to figure out where you are now, you have to figure out where you have been. What's your story? What have been the turning points in your life? I had a major turning point the day I stood up in the bus and told those snobby kids what they could do with their mean songs and taunting. That decision would change the person I was, even though it took me a few years to live out.

If I hadn't chosen to transfer schools, I might never have developed the confidence to go to modeling classes and try out for cheerleading. Because I did, I learned I had a knack and a love for dance and creating routines, which propelled me forward in the fitness field. This same love is what helps me create fun and motivating workouts for the people I train today.

Although I had many disappointments while growing up, I learned to turn them into positives. My desire for a healthy family that began in those years has fed the dream of the family I have today with my husband and his family. In fact, his dad is so much like my dad, it's scary.

As you will see in the upcoming chapters, I made some major mistakes in later years looking to find this closeness, but by learning from those mistakes and tragedies I have reached the peaceful place I'm in today with my husband and kids.

Don't let mistakes hold you back. Choose to make a change, and make them lessons to propel your life forward. Let those things make you stronger and more resilient, not make you settle for less out of life.

> Every person, all the events of your life, are there because you have drawn them there. What you choose to do with them is up to you.
>
> Richard Bach

A PERSONAL SUCCESS INVENTORY

Why did you pick up this book? Most people come to me because they want to lose weight or get into better shape. If it is one of those things, I know I can help you—but I also believe being overweight or a bit out of shape is probably not the most important change you need to make.

More often than not, our physical condition is a symptom of other things in our lives needing to be realigned. Once you understand what those things are, not only will it be easier to get the weight off, but it will also be more likely that you'll keep it off. The truth of the matter is, looking good in your "little black dress" will not make you fulfilled in life. What will is finding the best way to motivate yourself to keep pursuing your dream, whether it's running a marathon or having enough energy to keep up with your grandkids.

I also want to let you in on a little secret: *I don't have all of the answers for you.* Now, don't throw the book away before you let me explain. I have never had a personal training client who didn't have all of the answers already hidden within them; they just needed help organizing those answers. I know the same is true for you.

What keeps most people from their goals is very simply a lack of *motivation*. In general, people lack the motivation to pursue their dreams, or to persistently chase after them until they are achieved. As a rule, very few people have a weight or fitness problem; most suffer from a motivation problem in one form or another.

A lack of motivation tends to result from not having a workable plan suited for you. My goal is that by the end of this book, you will have one that will help you not only achieve your fitness goals but every other goal you have ever dreamed of achieving.

It all begins with choosing to make a change. But before we can start the next thirty days to a new you, we need to figure out where you want to end up, how this will look, and what has made you successful and fulfilled in the past. To learn these things about yourself, take a few minutes to respond to these questions:

1 What changes do you want to make, and why do you feel you need to make them?

Think for a moment what you hope your change in fitness and/or appearance will accomplish for you. Don't just get into the *what* you hope to change but also the *why* behind it. What other areas of your life would be affected? Explore why you are seeking change in those areas as well.

_____

_____

_____

_____

_____

2 What do you already do to accomplish those goals?

You may already be doing something you can build on to achieve your goals. What resources do you have on hand? Is there a gym where you work or local facilities you can take advantage of? How active are you now? What exercise are you already getting? How might you take it up a notch?

_____

_____

_____

_____

_____

3 What do you *like* to do?

A new program won't work if it doesn't fit in with what you enjoy doing. What activities make you feel good about yourself as a person? It could be something you are doing presently or something you used to do when you were younger.

_____

_____

_____

_____

_____

This last point is so important. As I have said, something already in you, not something imposed on you, is what will see you through. Maybe you were a cheerleader in high school, or maybe you love to dance. Did you play a team sport like basketball, volleyball, or soccer? Or did you participate in an individual sport like tennis or track? Do you like to run? Or do you enjoy long, leisurely walks with time to think about your life? Do you ever take hikes in the mountains or the woods? Do you have a dog you should walk more often? Or do you like to ride bikes with your family?

There are dozens of other things I'm sure you can think of, but you get the idea. What enjoyable pursuit from your past could be a catalyst for being active now? The best place to start is where you left off. I don't know very many people who, if they have never been runners before, will wake up one day and decide to start running without eventually losing heart and quitting. (This is why there are athletic clubs and personal trainers. Most of us need support to stay active, not to mention some instruction and coaching.)

However, when we consciously pursue what we've enjoyed in the past, we're much more likely to stick with it. For example, if you were a volleyball player in high school, I suggest checking into playing with a local adult volleyball league in your city. Or if you don't want to sign up for league play right away, there are always recreational options available. Find out when and where folks are getting together to practice in a low-key, social setting. Not only will this get you active again, but when you are ready to compete, you will have the drive to get in better shape off the court to increase your competitive edge on the court.

If you like dancing, maybe there are adult dance or Jazzercise classes you can participate in. There is no limit to the variety of dancercise-type classes available, from salsa to Bollywood to Nia to Zumba, just to name a few. Look around for a good fit for you.

Depending on your interests, you can look for an adult basketball, softball, bowling, tennis, or ultimate Frisbee league, or join a running, hiking, biking, climbing, kayaking, or skiing club. You name it, there is someone out there doing it. And if not, then there are probably others who would join a group if you started one.

> There are two primary choices in life: to accept conditions as they exist, or accept responsibility for changing them.
>
> Denis Waitley

LEARN WHAT YOU LOVE

You see, a lot of people think about getting in shape again, but then they try to do something they're not good at or they don't really like. Sure, running is a great exercise, but not all of us like to run. Some people love the long, solitary road stretching out for miles ahead and wouldn't miss a day of running for the world. But what about those of us who aren't wired like that?

Maybe you only love to run when you're chasing something like a Frisbee or a ball. You wouldn't jog around the block to save your life, but you could run miles on the basketball or tennis court.

Maybe you don't like competitive sports, so a good yoga, Pilates, spin, or strength-training class may more likely motivate you to get active.

Maybe you loathe the idea of working out alone and need the camaraderie of a group.

The question is what motivates *you*? Think about this as you decide which exercise is right for you.

I know a couple who both wanted to lose weight, so they tried to find a class they could go to together. That didn't work so well. He couldn't take the step classes, and she didn't like the ones resembling high school calisthenics.

However, they both enjoyed tennis, so they went to separate exercise classes but also played tennis together when they could. Had they tried to force one class or the other on each other, someone would have quit. But because they did what they loved, both lost weight. They also dramatically improved their tennis game (and probably some other areas in their marriage as well!).

The key is to discover, or rediscover, what you love doing and use it as a basis to get active again. It may not be exactly the same activity, but you can find something to fulfill the same drives in your personality. You just have to figure out what gets your motor running. Let what you love—or once loved—overcome your fear of doing it.

By choosing to do the positive things you love, the pleasure you feel will ultimately reinforce your commitment to continue. When your choices line up with your core desires, your brain actually releases a hormonelike chemical called dopamine, which controls the areas of the brain responsible for desire, decision making, and motivation.

When you engage in activities you enjoy, your brain discharges a surge of dopamine that begins to carve new neural pathways, reinforcing your desire to do them again. The key is to consistently choose positive activities that move you closer to who you want to be.

> Without passion you don't have energy; without energy, you have nothing.
>
> Donald Trump

REDIRECT YOUR CRAVINGS

Working out is not the only important change you need to choose to make. What you put into your body is *at least* as important as what you *do* with your body. Without the proper fuel, your engine won't feel like running anywhere. You'll just idle on the sofa.

What *do* you crave? What unhealthy cravings are you feeding, and which healthy ones are you starving? Do you crave clean foods or toxic ones? I cannot overstate the fact that you really are what you eat. As simple as this may sound, it's true.

If you want to be fit and vibrant, you have to eat fit and vibrant foods. Fit foods haven't had all of their nutritional value stripped away through processing. They are real, authentic, whole foods rather than artificial, factory-made, or factory-farmed foods.

Fit salmon, for example, fight their way upstream rather than languishing in the stagnant waters of a fish farm. Fit cows and chickens freely roam and forage for their own grass and seed rather than being confined their whole lives in tight stalls and cages. Fit foods are clean foods that haven't been contaminated with preservatives and flavor enhancers or weakened by additives and fillers or, in the case of produce, modified genetically.

To be fit, you need to eat fit foods. So the next thing you must consider in your personal success inventory is what you are eating.

4   What's in your cupboards, pantry, and refrigerator?

_____

_____

_____

Take a good look. Be honest. How many cartons, containers, boxes, and bags of prepared foods are sitting in your freezer and cupboards? Not to mention high-calorie, high-fat, high-sodium, high-sugar, *low-nutrition* snack items, such as chips, cookies, cereal bars, and, yes, all of those tasty crackers.

For any fitness program to work, you need to make sure you do have what you need and don't have what you don't need—and especially not what you are tempted by. One of the main reasons we as Americans are so overweight is that many of us have gotten used to processed foods because they are convenient. We gravitate toward foods that are usually sodium- and carb-packed or loaded with high fructose corn syrup (check out those energy drinks!) and contain things we need a doctorate in chemistry to pronounce. We will naturally eat what is quick and easy to prepare, so make sure you have the right foods on hand and have recipes that allow you to prepare healthy food quickly and easily.

The truth of the matter is that the best foods are the simplest, foods in their natural state that you don't even have to cook. Natural foods like fruits and vegetables should be your snacks of choice rather than refined, starchy foods like chips and crackers.

Beyond this, as I mentioned, your meals should consist of clean foods. Many people call these "whole foods" because they are all natural (beware: this is an overused claim; double-check the source), not modified in any way, and grown or raised in a toxic-free environment. Clean foods have been defined as "foods free of artificial preservatives, coloring, irradiation, synthetic pesticides, fungicides, ripening agents, fumigants, drug residues, and growth hormones."[3] Some examples of clean foods are Ezekiel bread and spelt tortillas or foods that are simply simple, such as steamed broccoli or grilled chicken breast without the cheese sauce or the injected flavor boosters.

If you want to transform yourself, you will need to transform your kitchen. Lasting transformation begins from the inside out, beginning with what you put inside your body. Out with the bad and in with the good. And don't just eat through the bad stuff before you fill your kitchen with good stuff. Clean out your cupboards now. Don't think twice. Don't take a second look at that open bag of chips or half-full box of ice cream bars. If you can't throw it away, give it to a shelter. Make a clean break.

If you have a favorite snack, like tortilla chips, lurking about when you feel just a little hungry or restless, chances are you will grab a handful without even thinking

---

3. Marian Burros, "Eating Well; A New Goal Beyond Organic: 'Clean Food,'" *The New York Times*, February 7, 1996.

instead of reaching for a carrot. However, if all you have in the house are carrots, your chances of reaching for a carrot are very good. Even though I will talk about setting up a meal plan later, for now I want you to start thinking about bringing more clean foods into your home to replace the processed—yes, toxic—foods.

COACHING MOMENT: MY CLIENT JEN

Jen loved soda. Not diet soda, but fully-loaded soda—*and* sweet chai lattes. After months of training and then reaching the hated plateau, she started to crave the sugary sodas and sweetened lattes she had given up. How could I help her redirect her unhealthy cravings?

I found Jen a replacement for her chai latte, a coffee drink with half the calories and sugar. I found something with similar flavors she could find at Starbucks, where she bought her chai. Instead of forbidding the treat, we exchanged it for something healthier.

Instead of her usual six regular sodas each week, I asked her if she could cut back to three diet sodas. She said she could. Fortunately, because she's not a big fan of diet soda, it did not become a habit but did give her a replacement. She is now down to a half cup of diet soda once a week when she craves that carbonated sugary taste.

Instead of enforcing an abrupt change, I researched viable options for her. I then explained how to realistically incorporate and apply the options. She has achieved both goals, having redirected both of her worst cravings. She is proud of herself and has gained a new momentum in her training.

Remember: Your destiny is not by chance—it is by choice. Set yourself up for success by intentionally choosing to make a change. Author and *Biggest Loser* host Jillian Michaels has this to say about the importance of every choice you make:

> Everything in life is a choice. From the moment we wake up and decide what kind of mood we're in, to the final choice we make as to whether to floss our teeth at night, we're making decisions all the time. Some choices are conscious and some are not, but the only way to live your dreams is to master the art of conscious choice making.[4]

Tell me what you eat; I'll tell you who you are.

Anthelme Brillat-Savarin

WHERE TO START TODAY

I want to encourage you to start making one specific choice every day that will keep you on track—and I'll tell you what it is. It is something you can start doing today that will create a winning habit and put you in the right frame of mind from the moment you get out of bed in the morning. It will set the stage for you to be motivated in the spirit of strength right from the beginning.

What is that choice? It is simply to do this: when you get up each morning, I want you to do a set of push-ups. I know what you're thinking. *No way. I hate push-ups.* A lot of people, especially women, find push-ups to be extremely difficult. That's why you will start with as many as you can do and work up from there. Even if you can only do them from your knees or leaning against the counter, I encourage you to do that until you are strong enough to do a regular push-up. The important thing is to start where you are and be consistent with doing whatever you can now *every single day.* Before you know it, you will be strong enough to do one regular push-up—then five, then ten,

4. Jillian Michaels, *Making the Cut: The 30-Day Diet and Fitness Plan for the Strongest, Sexiest You* (New York: Three Rivers Press, 2007), 11.

then twenty. You will be surprised how quickly you grow stronger—and how strong you will grow.

At eighteen, I started doing push-ups every morning in the Navy. I have done them every day of my life since, more for the emotional strength than for the physical strength it gives me. To me, the act of getting up and choosing to do push-ups at the start of each day represents honor, courage, and commitment.

My clients choose to do them each day for the same reason and to start the day with a healthy and fit mind-set. It has been a key factor in helping them lay a solid foundation for the rest of their day.

But here is another key: You must do them *correctly*. I would rather you do too few push-ups with good form than a bunch of sloppy ones while thinking you are accomplishing something. The purpose is not only to get you in the mind-set of strength but also to dramatically improve your core strength.

A solid, real push-up with good form is an example of using CORE STRENGTH because it causes you to fully engage your entire body and mind, to mentally dial in to the movement by engaging every muscle from the top of your head to the tips of your toes. It is an exercise in mind over matter—more specifically, mind over muscle. It forces you to tap into your innermost power and your deepest CORE STRENGTH.

Maybe all you can do now are five modified push-ups, or maybe two regular push-ups and eight modified ones. Maybe you can start with more. The important thing is making the choice to begin and then to be consistent. If you have difficulty attempting a traditional push-up due to an injury or other physical challenges, try doing push-ups while leaning against a counter with your feet out behind you. Keep your back, neck, torso, and hips perfectly aligned all the way up and down.

⭐ ⭐ ⭐

COACHING MOMENT: MY CLIENT LUGINIA

Luginia came to me as a sixty-two-year-old with diabetes and a prior history of back surgery and knee pain. Before discussing what she could *not* do, our first discussion revolved around what she does do, what she can do, and what she feels good about. I discovered she walks most nights for two miles and then is wiped out for at least twenty minutes. I encouraged her to rest for twenty minutes after her walk and then walk one more mile on her treadmill while watching the evening news.

I was also able to show her that just because she could not get down on her knees and onto the floor didn't mean she couldn't do a push-up. She learned how to do push-ups against her countertop.

By adding these new components to her program and to her life, she has decreased her insulin intake, lost twenty pounds, and can consistently do *all* of the workouts I plan for her without any problems.

If Luginia can do her push-ups every day, so can you!

I want you to get up in the morning and do however many push-ups you can, but I want you to do them with an attitude of excellence, which will be reflected in every other decision you make throughout your day. Do them in a way that tells the world, "Laziness and sloppiness have no control over me." Do them in a way that pushes you to do your best in everything. Do them with the resolve of knowing this is the first habit in forming the new you, the person you want to be and you know you are capable of becoming.

> When you actively align your choices with your life's purpose and goals, you live more honestly, more courageously, and with a greater integrity, and these virtues bring with them a powerful kind of freedom.
>
> Zoe Weil

IT'S YOUR CHOICE

Remember: To establish a strong CORE, the first step is to *choose* to make a change. So, what kind of choices will you make? Will you choose to get up and do your push-ups every day, to eat nothing but clean foods, and to be happy? Believe it or not, you do have those options. If you wake up in the morning with a frown on your face, I want you to choose to smile instead. Say, "I will be happy today. Today will be a good day." Lift up your head and believe that no matter what's thrown at you, you will choose to handle it with grace and joy.

If you're having some trouble with your relationships or if you're simply feeling disconnected from the ones you love, choose to make a change. Tell someone you love them, or write an unexpected note of thanks. It will make you feel better.

When you step onto the floor in the morning, choose to be healthy and happy and grateful. Choose to get down and do your push-ups. Get up and look at yourself in the mirror and say you love yourself and your family enough to be the best you can be. Start your day by making different and better choices, and let those choices set you on the course to a stronger and fitter life.

It's up to you to choose to make a change.

> Until a person can say deeply and honestly, "I am what I am today because of the choices I made yesterday," that person cannot say, "I choose otherwise."
>
> Stephen R. Covey

Life doesn't hand us excuses.

It hands us lessons.

CHAPTER 2
OWN WHERE YOU ARE NOW

> A man should know himself like the palm of his hand, know the exact number of his defects and qualities, know how far he can go, foretell his failures, be what he is. And, above all, accept these things.
>
> Albert Camus

From the time I was eight years old when my dad had that talk with me about choosing my destiny, to the time I chose to stand up for myself on the bus, to the time I chose to be the best me I could be in high school, choices changed my life. I quickly realized I was able to make choices that would impact the direction of my life. My future was not just about luck. My destiny would never be determined by my circumstances but by my choices. Learning I could choose the course of my life from early on gave me a sense of power. Unfortunately, I have learned both the good and the bad side of that. In my teens, for example, I made some horrendously bad choices. All of my choices—good and bad—have made me the person I am today. I can't look back and change anything, but I can own my many mistakes, as well as my occasional triumphs, and learn from them.

To establish a strong CORE, not only must we *choose* to make a change. We must also learn to *own* where we are now because of all of the choices that have led us here. No matter what your past looks like, it won't do you much good except as a learning tool to take you one step closer to where you want to be in the future. Yesterday may have put you where you are now, but the choices you make today will move you either closer or farther away from where you want to be tomorrow. Look at your past, own it, learn from it, and then get back to work. Today is a brand-new day; use it to make a brand-new tomorrow.

As I've mentioned, if you choose to get up every morning to do your push-ups, you are already on the way to where you want to be. If you start your day right, you are more likely to end it right as well. As the saying goes, "Well begun is half done." As you go through your day, choose to make a change in your perspective. Find the positive in the negatives. Focus on the strength you are building to overcome your weaknesses; then find opportunities to take advantage of them.

Let me ask you this. What do you want from your life? Are you living your dream? What can you do to get there?

Reaching your destiny is about little changes of habit, which begin with deliberately owning where you are and choosing to do the right things to change. Which is easier: Hating who you are and continuing to do the things that make you unhappy with yourself? Or changing your habits to become the person you would love to be? Surprisingly, little changes create big results. It never ceases to thrill me when clients are surprised by some change—either in their energy, their outlook, or their abs—from the smallest lifestyle adjustments.

The key is consistency. You may feel like the tortoise now, but stick with the program and you will be as fit as the hare in no time. You will be smarter, too, because you have learned to press through to the end of the race instead of lying around, thinking someday your ship will come in all on its own.

> Accept yourself as you are. Otherwise you will never see opportunity.
> You will not feel free to move toward it; you will feel you are
> not deserving.
>
> Maxwell Maltz

UNREADY FOR SUCCESS

By the time I was in ninth grade, I was starting to bloom as a young woman. The Prince Valiant haircut was gone, I was carrying myself with more confidence, I had learned how to use makeup correctly, and I was no longer that awkward little sixth grader facing down constant teasing. What I hadn't learned yet, however, was that real beauty emerges from the inside out. That lesson would take me some time to understand.

As I have already said, by the end of ninth grade I had the confidence to try out for cheerleading and made it onto the squad. What I didn't tell you was that the school I was now attending was also the high school where all of those snooty private school kids were attending. That's right. I had made the ugly-duckling-to-swan transformation in front of the very same kids whom I had told off that day on the bus. Amazingly, several of those kids from the private school were the same ones who befriended me once I made the cheer squad.

Still, my stars were far from aligned. Soon after I made the squad, my dad learned he was being transferred again. Choosing popularity over family, I made arrangements to stay with my aunt and uncle and cousins instead of moving to Georgia with Dad and Peggy. This way, I could continue at the same school my sophomore year.

My new home was very different from the ones I'd known. While I love my dad and stepmother and have learned a lot from them, my aunt and uncle's family had a closeness I had not found and did not know again until my marriage to Scott.

My cousins didn't go to the same high school I did but to a private Christian school. My hanging with the in crowd, partying, and doing whatever I wanted did not sit well with their family values. Honestly, I was a rebel and a little full of myself. When push came to shove, I was a pretty bad example for my cousins, and it wasn't long before my aunt and uncle asked my parents to take me back.

I had tasted a little independence from my parents, however, and I didn't want to let it go. So when my grandmother in Oklahoma City offered to take me in, I jumped at the opportunity. I'm sure she felt she could keep me out of trouble, so she offered to buy me a car if I came and lived with her. I didn't have to think twice about that one!

Once again, I would be starting school in one place and finishing the year in another. By the end of the first semester, I was headed for Oklahoma City to move in with my grandparents.

Toward the end of the year my grandparents left me alone in the house for the weekend, and I performed the ultimate teenager miscalculation: I invited a few friends over for a party, and half the school showed up. It was far beyond anything I could control.

My grandparents were fairly wealthy and collected art and photography. No matter how hard I tried to clean up and cover my tracks, I couldn't repair the things that had been damaged. Then, worst of all, my grandparents found some used condoms in their bedroom. They assumed the worst—that they were mine, *which they weren't*—but my attitude didn't exactly convince them otherwise. I defiantly insisted I had done nothing wrong. So I found myself packing yet again.

I was convinced by now that I could take care of myself. So after being sent to Georgia to live with my parents, I made plans to move back to Oklahoma City. I did not want anyone looking over my shoulder or telling me what to do, so I lied about being able to live with a friend and her family over the school year. I talked one of my girlfriends into pretending she was her mom and calling my dad. She told him I was welcome to stay the year with them so I could continue at the same school. I am not sure how my parents ever agreed to that, but by the time my junior year was starting, I was on my way back to Oklahoma City.

This choice was absolutely insane. I spent the first weekend and the first couple of days of school with my friend who had posed as her mother. After we registered, got our books, and then started classes, I pawned everything I had of value and bought a four-door Ford Granada.

Then reality sank in. I couldn't stay with my friend's family any longer under the ruse that I was just spending a few nights, so I left with nowhere else to go. That night I slept in my car. The next day I snuck into the gym early, showered and dressed, and went to class. I did the same thing every night and morning for the next six weeks.

Even though I'd made the choices to do these things, I was incredibly angry with my parents for allowing me to return to Oklahoma. I resented that they were so clueless, and it took me years to forgive their carelessness. In retrospect, I realize I was testing them in my own way and, from my perspective at that time, they utterly failed.

This was a pretty low point in my life, and I am lucky I made it through without falling into some real trouble. As it was, I ended up as a manager in training at a pizza place and then renting a room from a pregnant prostitute whose ex-pimp kept hitting on me to "take up the work." Fortunately, although I was in a bad place, what my father had built into me over the years kept me from the deep end. I managed to steer clear of his advice, as well as his advances.

Then, low of lows, my car was struck from behind while I was driving. I wasn't hurt, but my car was totaled. Unable to drive to work anymore, I lost my room and threw myself at the mercy of my classmate's family, who took me in and let me stay in her room. My classmate looked like Marilyn Monroe and had a meticulously organized closet, which I was not allowed to get near. She had a double bed, but I was grateful for the space on her floor to rest every night. I don't think I ever realized how strange it was that I was allowed to move in with this family. I'm amazed that complete strangers could take me in and not expect anything in return. (People will always surprise you.)

My friend "Marilyn" would sneak out regularly to go to parties, and I remember lying in her room unable to sleep because I was terrified her parents would come in and I'd have to explain where she was. The worst thing about it was that she always wanted me to go with her. At first I refused, afraid to get into any more trouble, but when she kept getting away with it, I finally agreed to go one night. Wouldn't you know it—that night her parents checked the room. When we got home, my friend cried and said I'd made her go.

It wasn't long before I was on a plane headed to Dad's house. I finished my junior year at yet another school and lived with Dad and Peggy in Norcross, Georgia.

I began my senior year determined I would make a change, but unfortunately I wasn't determined enough. I was soon hanging out with the party crowd again. We started making fake IDs to get into bars and nightclubs, all using my grandparents' address because it was the only out-of-state address anyone could get ahold of. (Once, the police broke up a party and everyone had IDs with this same address.)

This led to the lowest point of my life. Using the fake ID, I went into a bar to dance and drink. As the evening wore on, one guy started paying a little more attention to me, and before long we were making out on the dance floor. He was a little too handsy, but I was tipsy and loving the attention. When he and his buddies were getting ready to leave, he invited me to come along and party with them. Naively I thought he must have really liked me, so I went. But as we got to their van, they suddenly forced me inside, held me down, covered my mouth, and blindfolded me.

The next couple of hours were so horrible that I can't even talk about them. They raped me one by one. When they were done, they drove me to the front of my house and tossed me out on the grass.

The next month was just as horrible, as I found out I was pregnant, had an abortion, and returned to school trying to act as if nothing had happened. My dad was supportive, but my stepmom and I didn't see eye-to-eye on the abortion, and because of her perpetual condemnation, we could no longer live in the same house.

I moved out, got an apartment, held a series of part-time jobs, and finished my senior year at Norcross High. This was the first year I started and finished at the same school since fifth grade, but it was also the worst year of my life.

> Never allow yourself to be made a victim. Accept no one's definition of your life; define yourself.
>
> Harvey Fierstein

YES, THAT WAS ME

To look at me today, you wouldn't know I had spent the greater part of my high school career living on my own, living out of my car, or going through some of those harrowing experiences. Looking back, I can't really believe I was able to finish high school without any interruptions, other than changing schools and living arrangements every year.

I'm not proud of many of the decisions I made during this time in my life, but I won't deny they happened. I know that but for the grace of God, I wouldn't be here today. For all of the good things that happened to me growing up, I have discovered the value of looking back and fully owning the bad things as well. Those things, more than anything else, make me cherish my family, my work, and the other important relationships I have today. It makes the good things all the sweeter and also makes me realize there are no lows I can't bounce back from. I have been through some of the worst things life can throw at a person and have not just survived—I've thrived.

The only way I have been able to do this is by owning every bit of it. As Albert Einstein once said, "Once we accept our limits, we go beyond them." The truth is, until you own your mistakes and limitations, you'll never move forward to reach your next level of success.

I have learned the tremendous value of looking back. I wasn't always able to because I was afraid. I always wanted—and still want—to be strong. I felt that looking into the eye of what scared me the most would break me. It was a struggle at first, but now I always try to learn from the decisions I've made and the things that have happened to me.

Looking back is what allows you to own the situation and the fear, and that ownership allows you to grow and get past it. I try to teach people to do this because most of us don't naturally want to own our bad decisions along with the good. Yet how will we ever change what's happening to us if we keep following the same patterns and habits that put us where we are now?

The best teacher is experience. Don't neglect to learn from your very own life lessons.

Look back and find some mistake, some tragedy, something you regret. There is a lesson to be learned there. Maybe you made a decision you wouldn't again. Or perhaps you would, but now that you know how to count the cost, you'd do things differently to make the choice less painful for everyone involved.

I look back at some of my decisions and shake my head, wondering, *What could I possibly have been thinking?* But I also embrace those moments, as painful as some of them are, and learn from them. Then those choices, instead of being negatives dragging me down, empower me to shape my future into something better for my family and myself. They give me the resolve to stick to the right decisions and work through the hard times, which is so much better than giving up.

What I want is on the other side of the hard, humbling work; it's not back where I was before, so I'll stick to the plan and see it through. There is no going back to change things. After all, where you end up is more important than where you've been. In the words of Victorian novelist Mary Anne Evans, commonly known by her pen name, George Eliot, "It is never too late to be who you might have been."

> The curious paradox is that when I accept myself just as I am, then I can change.
>
> Carl Rogers

THERE IS ONLY ONE YOU

Let's say a friend comes over to get ready with you for a party or a special night out. She goes into your closet, pulls something off the rack, and in a voice of mock horror says, "Is this yours?" What will you say? Will you artfully dodge the issue and say, "No, my mom left it," or will you say, "Yeah, it's mine," even though you feel the same way she does about it?

The thing is, if you dodge the issue, she will put the item back and you'll both forget about it. That outdated, horrific garment will likely hang there for the rest of your life or until the house burns down or you move out or the roof caves in. However, if you can admit it's yours—"Yes, it's mine!"—you can *do* something about it. After your friend leaves, you can say to yourself, "Okay, I just *owned* the fact that I *own* this. Now let me take responsibility for what I do with it. I haven't worn this thing for years, it's ugly, and I won't wear it ever again. I don't know why I keep it around, so I'm getting rid of it." You can put it in a sack, hopefully with every other thing you haven't worn for years, and give it all to charity.

For you, it might sound something like this: "I love those pants, but I can't fit into them anymore. I don't want to give them away, but why hang on to them if they don't fit? I need to either let the seams *out* or bring my hips *in*." Once you've *owned* them (and the size of your hips), you can decide what you *do* about them.

In the same way you own the pants, you need to own who you are now—the good, the bad, and the ugly. Once you own it, you can begin to work toward improving it. Until then, nothing will change. If you say to yourself, "Oh, I've just put on a little weight after my pregnancy; it's natural and to be expected," then you are not owning the shape you're in. You're just making excuses. You need to look at where you are and be honest with yourself. What is good about your body? What do you want to change?

COACHING MOMENT: MY CLIENT SUSAN

A young mother named Susan had let herself gain far too much weight after having two children in under a year apart. She had lost her energy, drive, and identity. She would not let her husband see her naked with the lights on, she had to wear support undergarments, and she was horrified when her one-year-old called her fat. She was tired and depressed and didn't look at all like the woman her husband had married. One day she realized she had to make a change.

This initial step is often the hardest, because accepting one's own faults can feel demoralizing. Once Susan came to terms with her situation, she could take the next step and analyze the problem, along with its causes and some potential solutions. She was able to talk about when she felt the best in her life, and what she thought had taken place from then until now. After taking time to write down her thoughts, she looked at her situation in a more tangible way rather than interpreting the problem on a purely emotional level.

Susan became painfully aware of her declining fitness. Her children noticed, her husband noticed, and finally she noticed. She came to terms with the problem and made a decision to identify the root causes and alternative solutions. Upon reviewing her options, she decided on action steps to move toward success.

To be continued . . .

Before you do anything, you need to own your whole self, the bad and the good. Maybe your abdomen is protruding a little, but you have a great rear end. Be proud of that great backside. Move forward and work on your abs, but also appreciate what you have goin' on that's lookin' good!

Own everything about yourself. Accept the reality that perhaps you eat or drink too much or have certain habits you need to change. If you don't take hold of the things bothering you, you'll never be able to deal with them. If you are in constant denial, those issues will continue to exist but you will have no power over them. When you own the things that belong to you, then you will have the motivation to choose what to do with them.

In his article "The Power to Change," Marshall Goldsmith interviews Tim Irwin, author of *Run With the Bulls Without Getting Trampled*, about what motivates and sustains change. Irwin explains it this way:

We don't lose weight by looking in the mirror, but it does get the ball rolling. It galvanizes our attention. At that juncture, we can affirm the feedback or deny it. . . .

. . . Denial perpetuates the status quo, while affirmation opens the door for the possibility of change.[5]

Irwin suggests that the people who succeed in life are the ones who take ownership of their entire situation, the forces working *for* and *against* their efforts to change. They continually evaluate and reevaluate what is strengthening and weakening their efforts.

This evaluation requires a degree of mindfulness and self-reflection; it requires looking in the mirror—a full-length mirror—every day. Yes, *always* look in a full-length mirror before you walk out the door. And, yes, people *do* look at your feet.

No matter who you are, some things are already in place to get you where you want to be with how you look, how you carry yourself, and how you feel about yourself. Owning who you are is the first step toward truly loving yourself.

> Self-love has very little to do with how you feel about your outer self. It's about accepting all of yourself. You've got to learn to accept the fool in you as well as the part that's got it going on.
>
> Tyra Banks

ADDRESSING BASIC ISSUES

A few years back, I wanted to add to my knowledge base to better help people as a trainer and motivator, so I started working on a second degree in sociology. During this time, I started studying the work of Abraham Maslow and Howard Gardner and making my own connections between psychology, motivational theory, and wellness.

I also started taking a deeper look inside, or a wider look in the mirror, and recognizing

---

5. Tim Irwin as quoted by Marshall Goldsmith, "The Power to Change," *Bloomberg Businessweek*, April 11, 2007, http://www.businessweek.com/careers/content/apr2007/ca20070411_924286.htm (accessed May 1, 2009).

the effect I had on other people, either good or bad. I realized I would never be fully liberated to be the best I could be until I freed myself from the weights of the past.

The process I envisioned is very similar to what people go through in twelve-step programs when they must own past choices and apologize for whatever harm they've caused others. By doing this, they achieve a sense of closure so that they can let go of the past. The owning, the closure, and the letting go are all part of getting to the next stage of life.

Not taking ownership is where the disconnect happens. You can't learn from a mistake until you own it. We will all make some blunders. The earlier we own them, rather than continuing to live in denial, the sooner we can get on with our lives and begin to live honestly with ourselves.

I made some bad decisions when I was eighteen, but I didn't own those mistakes. Because of that, I didn't start experiencing breakthroughs and moving forward in some major areas, both personally and professionally, until I was thirty-eight.

I made a decision to move in with my grandmother, instead of my parents when I left my aunt and uncle's home. This decision led me to some bad choices but allowed me to develop the relationship with my grandmother that I will cherish for a lifetime. So from the bad came good.

I have to own it all, even the decision to have that party, and the worse decision to not apologize after I was caught. Had I been able to own each decision at the time, things would have been so different for me.

Instead, for a year or so I ran from my mistakes and was too proud to admit I was making the wrong kinds of choices. I told people, "Yeah, that was a great party," as if I had really accomplished something in life, and at the same time I was living out of my car and off of everyone else's kindness. Now I have to ask myself, *What was that about?*

Not owning my errors then put me at risk for all kinds of problems far worse than any mistake I had made in the first place. It launched me into situations that could have permanently barred me from the dreams I am only starting to live today.

Renowned psychologist Carl Jung once stated, "We cannot change anything until we accept it." It is so simple, so true, yet, to many of us, so elusive.

It took me twenty years to accept my mistakes. I still wonder how far behind my mistakes have put me. Although I will never know, I do know I can't let them delay me any longer. I can only own them, accept where they have brought me, and then take advantage of the opportunity to change.

A few years back, I finally called my grandmother and apologized for what I had done to her house and her trust. It was a great time of reconciliation and forgiveness, and now my grandmother is one of my greatest allies.

It doesn't always work this way, though. Many folks won't return the goodwill when you try to reconcile with them. Others may let you back into their lives to a limited extent, but there will never be complete trust or respect. Sometimes this happens. The important thing is to get the weight off of your shoulders by making the effort to ask others for forgiveness. If they still want to carry the burden, that's their call. Just make sure you set *yourself* free.

Is there something in your life you regret having done? Shedding extra baggage isn't always about losing weight or cleaning out your closet; sometimes it's about letting go of old hurts and past mistakes. Preparing the way for a successful and fit life starts within you. Identifying with who you are, what you represent, and what defines you inside gives way to a framework for a solid foundation to build your life upon. Check your foundations. Don't let a crack go ignored; sooner or later it will cause the walls to crumble.

What is it that you regret? What will you do about it? Do you need to make a phone call or go see someone? Maybe you need to write a letter to yourself and formally apologize for the mistakes you've made in the past that have set you back.

How will you facilitate your own healing and use your past as a tool to create change?

> You are wholly complete, and your success in life will be in direct proportion to your ability to accept this truth about you.
>
> Dr. Robert Anthony

Stand Like You Own It

Ownership is a mind-set. It is creating change from the inside out. Your frame of mind determines how you frame your body. It's all about how you posture yourself.

One of the keys I learned from my longtime mentor Dr. Jack Barnathan is the importance of engaging what he calls your triad of power. This triad is comprised of your back, chest, and shoulders. Your back and chest represent two major muscle groups, and then you've got your shoulders, which bring alignment to your back and chest. If you are doing any kind of movement, such as a squat, lunge, or bicep curl, and your shoulders are not correctly aligned, you will be off all of the way down. That's how people create back problems. Once you set your triad of power in place, the rest of your body lines up where it needs to.

Always focus on keeping your shoulders back and down, as if you're sliding them into your back pockets. When I coach someone for any exercise position, I tell them, "Put your shoulders in your back pockets, draw your navel into your spine, rock your pelvis slightly forward, and place your feet shoulder-width apart."

Focus on your posture. Sit up straight. Stand up straight. Not only is it good for your muscles, but it's great for your outlook. Good posture will make you look younger and thinner, and when you have proper alignment, you're positioned to better handle the bumps and blows that come your way.

Hold your head up, pull your shoulders back, and take ownership of how you carry yourself. Be proud of who you are—and of who you are becoming.

It's time to move on and make a plan. Now that you have owned who you are and why you are where you are today, you can begin taking responsibility for making the changes that will get you where you want to go.

> Nobody can go back and start a new beginning, but anyone can start today and make a new ending.
>
> Maria Robinson

We learn and we live when we stumble and fall,
but with our strength inside, we will indeed stand tall.

I want you to believe in yourself and your spirit.
Grasp your dream—you have one. Own it and live it.
The power you need to make change and take charge
is part of your soul and part of your heart.

We each have our own special piece of the pie . . .
our gift, our purpose—it's all held inside.
It's great and you have it. Please know that you do.
What you bring to the table is unique and is true.

The beauty you have is both inside and out . . .
combined with your talents, a triple threat, no doubt.
Throw back your shoulders and hold your head high,
and look and find all your strength deep inside.

When times get tough—and they will; that's okay—
Look in the mirror. You know what to say.
"I'm strong. I have spirit. This too shall pass,
'Cause what I have inside me is so built to last."

—Staci

If you can't let your significant other see you before bed with the lights on,

it's a call for change.

REFINE YOUR VISION AND TAKE RESPONSIBILITY FOR YOUR DREAMS

CHAPTER 3

> Let us not seek to fix the blame for the past. Let us accept our own responsibility for the future.
>
> John F. Kennedy

Many people who own their past still aren't able to use it as a catalyst for change. Worse than "fixing blame," they use their own shortcomings as excuses to stay the same. Sure, they've owned it all, but now they are stuck "holding the bag," so to speak. Sometimes this place of acknowledgment can be as bad as the denial we are trying to leave behind.

You've learned that to establish a strong CORE, you must *choose* to make a change and *own* where you are now. The next step is to *refine* your vision and take *responsibility* for your dreams. In other words, you must envision and take responsibility for the next step *past* where you are now.

It is one thing to take ownership and another to take responsibility for doing something about what you own. Ownership is a thought process, a mind-set, a state of *being.* Responsibility, on the other hand, is an action. It is the ability to *respond* to your state of being. It is the initiative to take those old pants and actually do something with them—or with your body so it fits into them again.

Instead of complaining about the fact that something doesn't fit anymore or ignoring it altogether, *ownership* accepts the fact that your booty has blossomed. *Responsibility* then takes that information and makes a plan. Will you clear out all of those too-tight clothes and buy a new wardrobe? Then that's what you should plan to *do*. Throw *all* of those clothes out right now and get out your checkbook. If you can't afford a new wardrobe or aren't willing to give up ever wearing your old size again, then make a plan to burn more calories than you eat on a daily basis. Find a way to start and stick with a clean-eating and workout program. The point is to take responsibility and move forward.

> The key to accepting responsibility for your life is to accept the fact that your choices, every one of them, are leading you inexorably to either success or failure, however you define those terms.
>
> Neal Boortz

FINDING MY WAY:
ONE STEP FORWARD, TWO STEPS BACK

After high school, I got my first full-time job at All-State Business Systems. I was the switchboard operator and receptionist and soon found I had a knack for detail, organization, and taking creative initiative. It was my first experience working in a professional atmosphere, and I began to believe I could do more than work in a pizzeria or at the mall. Not only did I feel good about what I was doing, but the managers appreciated my work too and wanted to help develop my gifts and talents.

It makes such a difference to be surrounded by people who believe in you. Wow, was that a new experience for me! What I learned while working there is a big part of what has kept me moving forward ever since. My managers taught me that I could do whatever I set my mind to do. If I took responsibility for my future, despite all of the mistakes of my past, I could still propel myself toward whatever my heart told me I should be doing. They echoed and then revived the distant voice of my father, a voice which until then had quieted to a whisper.

Ten years earlier, my dad had told me, "Your destiny is not by chance—it is by choice." By now, life had buried those words so deep inside that I couldn't hear them anymore. By the time I was eighteen, I'd known three moms, transitioned through four high schools in as many different states, been evicted from six different homes, almost been lured into prostitution, been raped and then condemned by my stepmother for having had an abortion—and still these managers found great promise in me. Their belief in my potential revived my excitement about life.

I was the kid everybody had picked on. I was not pretty; we didn't have money. I was the kid with the depressing past who had every reason to not believe in herself. I had to be able to own all that had happened but at the same time not let it consume me. I moved past it. I had the choice of going down either the path of negativity or the path of possibility. I owned my past but also knew if things were going to change, it was up to me. It was my responsibility.

And I took that responsibility seriously. At All-State I kept working on becoming better at my job at the switchboard. I got very good at determining whether reps were in their offices and when it was best to take a message or patch clients through. I could stand up and look out the window to see each employee's car, so I knew when people were in the building. If they were in but didn't answer their phones, then I would page them over the intercom. I got so good at it that the managers eventually started giving me more responsibilities, such as dealing with accounts payable and receivable.

Through this experience, I learned how easy it is to work hard not only when you are motivated but also when you love the people you're working with. I am thankful to have been surrounded by people who encouraged my gifts while I was there. As I worked there, my confidence continued to increase.

With my confidence came a desire to go to college. Being on my own at the time, I realized the only way I could afford tuition would be if I joined the military. So I visited the recruiters and decided I wanted to become a Navy hospital corpsman because I thought it would be cool to work in a hospital. However, on the day I went to enlist, I was told I would be a mechanical engineer—because that's what they needed.

I wasn't sure what to do, but I knew it was my destiny to be a hospital corpsman, and I had no desire to learn how to be a mechanic. I also realized I hadn't signed up for anything yet and the Army and Air Force recruiting offices were just a few doors down. I remember standing there feeling a boldness rise within me, and I said, "Sir, I don't want to learn how to fix a toilet or a refrigerator. I want to be in the medical field. If I can't, then I won't join the Navy." I wasn't sure what would happen, and I really expected him to turn me away, but I knew my future was down this path with the same certainty that I had known it was time to find a new school when I was in sixth grade.

In the event that the recruiter said no, I didn't have a backup plan, but as it turned out I didn't need one. The officer looked at me, grumbled under his breath a bit, and said, "Okay, we can do that if that's the way you feel." Then he changed my paperwork on the spot. I signed and started getting my things together for boot camp.

In boot camp I learned to really push myself. If we were doing push-ups, I wanted to do the most or at least more than I'd done the day before. I was competitive, but it wasn't so much about competing with others as it was about competing with myself. I always believed in improving my personal best, knowing I had done everything I could that day to make me the best person I could be. It was about taking responsibility for what *I* could do to be the best *I* could be. Even after I got out of boot camp, this attitude stuck with me.

> If you take responsibility for yourself, you will develop a hunger to accomplish your dreams.
>
> Les Brown

PLAN AND PLAN AGAIN

However, I also learned that just because you make a quality decision doesn't mean there won't be setbacks. Navy recruits, I suppose like most young people when collected into one place, can be a rowdy bunch. Partying was something I hadn't cleared out of my system yet from high school, or at least I hadn't learned how to balance it with my commitments. I threw myself into it yet somehow got through boot camp. But during medical training school, it all caught up with me.

Let me preface this story by saying that from the beginning, I had my sights set on being an officer. I was always taking on extra responsibilities and looking to lead. I was determined to be the best I could be during my time in the service. Unfortunately, you can't have it both ways. Between extra work and too much partying, I ended up flunking an important hospital corps exam—so important that the rest of my class moved on without me. I had to retake almost everything.

This is also when I met Jimmy and fell passionately in love. It seemed as if everyone around us was getting married to different classmates, so it felt natural for us to do the same thing. I remember thinking, *Getting married must be the right thing to do. Everybody else is fulfilled and happy. They must be in love.* No one had really told me they loved me before, and when Jimmy said it, getting married seemed like the natural thing to do, even though we had only known each other a couple of months.

Well, as you guessed, no matter how right it felt, it wasn't. When Jimmy graduated, he was stationed in Oakland, California, and I was still in school in the Great Lakes restarting my training. I remember going to the pay phone in the lounge every night at seven to get his call, and then one night the phone didn't ring. It didn't ring the next night either. In fact, it didn't ring for a week. When we finally spoke again, he told me he had found someone else and was *really* in love this time.

I was crushed. I found out the hard way that just because everyone else is doing it, that doesn't make it right for me.

Demoralized, I did the only thing I knew to do: I threw myself into my classes and got through school. This time I passed, but instead of joining Jimmy in Oakland, I changed my orders and went to Bethesda, Maryland. Soon after, Iraq invaded Kuwait and America found itself sending troops to the Persian Gulf. I was assigned to the USNS *Comfort*, a mercy class hospital ship.

The war and all of the excitement of being deployed had changed my relationship with Jimmy. Since Jimmy was stationed next door on a sister hospital ship, it looked for a time as if he and I might get back together. After all, he decided, I was really, truly his number one girl. We made arrangements to see each other, and they were approved since neither of us had ever filed the divorce papers. I flew to see him on one of the Desert Duck helicopters.

For a brief time, our marriage flickered to life again. Even though we were stationed on different ships, we were able to keep in touch by letter, and from time to time we could type messages back and forth via the ship-to-ship communications set up for personal use. We didn't have e-mail then, so this was the closest thing to staying in touch "real time." Otherwise, I would start a letter every morning, add to it throughout the day, and then mail it just before going to bed.

I think today we miss something by not writing our loved ones on real paper that we can hold in our hands and keep in a drawer. Reading typed inscriptions on a computer screen just isn't the same. I wrote to Jimmy and my family daily and loved to hear from them. There was something special about hearing my name at mail call and carrying a real letter around all day and reading it repeatedly before sticking it back in my pocket. I even posted a piece of paper above my bunk that I'd write poetry on while I rested there between shifts and listened to Queen on my Walkman. (Remember cassette tapes? That seems like forever ago!)

As soon as the war was over, I returned to Bethesda and put in for a transfer to Oakland. Before I moved to California, Jimmy and I went to Texas, where I met his family. Things were still pretty up in the air, though, and when I returned to Bethesda and found out I was pregnant, I was more confused than happy about it. To make things even worse, I miscarried the baby. I wasn't sure what was happening with my body, my marriage, or my life. It was a very unsettling time of transition.

Finally my orders came through and I moved to Oakland, where Jimmy and I got an apartment and set up house together. Without the focus and excitement of the war, however, Jimmy's interests wandered again. So after about three months, I moved out of our apartment into the barracks at Treasure Island near Alcatraz, and we finally filed our divorce papers.

> Accept responsibility for your life. Know that it is you who will get you where you want to go, no one else.
>
> Les Brown

THE DIFFERENCE BETWEEN TAKING AND ACCEPTING RESPONSIBILITY

A lot of people equate owning something or taking responsibility to admitting they were at fault, but this is not the case. Certainly there are some things in life for which we are at fault, and we should *accept* the responsibility to fix those things. However, there are other times when we are not at fault but must still *take* responsibility for improving an unfortunate situation. If you don't take responsibility for what happens next in your life, who will? Your happiness is entirely your responsibility.

Business success guru Brian Tracy sums it up this way:

> The key to happiness is having a sense of control over what's going on in your life. The more you feel that you're in control, the happier you'll be. . . . The more responsibility you take, the more in control you are. . . . So there's a direct relationship between responsibility, control, freedom, and happiness. The happiest people in the world are those who feel absolutely terrific about themselves, and this is the natural outgrowth of accepting total responsibility for every part of their lives.[6]

---

6. Brian Tracy, "Taking Personal Responsibility," *SuccessMethods.org*, http://www.successmethods.org/brian_tracy-a19.html (accessed March 1, 2009).

I have learned that hidden in every problem is an opportunity for the person who's willing to take responsibility to find it. When I worked at All-State Business Solutions, problems occurred that I didn't create, but I found that when I took responsibility for solving them, my managers noticed and rewarded me for being part of the solution. I decided to take responsibility for issues no one else was willing to, and as a result, issues got resolved and I got promoted.

So when you go into your closet and can't find anything to wear because it is so disorganized, who will fix it if you don't take the responsibility? If you have junk food lying around your kitchen that trips you up whenever you are hungry, who will rectify the situation if you don't? Maybe you keep it around for your kids, but if you aren't training them to eat smarter, how will they be equipped to make better choices as adults or when they have families of their own? If not you, who will take the responsibility for ending the unhealthy cycle?

I've never heard of a kid who came home after a nutrition lesson in health class and said, "Mom, I really need to start eating healthier. Would you stop buying us ice cream and chips?" Frankly, I don't know very many adults who would say that either.

If things are going to change in your home, then someone has to take responsibility for it. Your kids won't do it and even though your spouse might, sitting around waiting for it to happen can be worse than watching grass grow. If things are going to get better, you have to take responsibility for your "domains"—your kitchen, your job, your closet, your daily routine, your checkbook and credit cards, and all of the areas in your life— by setting goals for how you want each of those areas to serve you. Then create a plan to achieve those goals.

> There is no such thing as insanity. There are only varying levels of irresponsibility.
>
> Thomas Szasz

REFINING YOUR VISION

Although we will talk more about goal setting in chapter five, I want you to start thinking now about what you want. To establish a strong CORE, I want you to start *refining* your vision along with taking *responsibility* for your dreams. What is the vision you hold of your best self? What do you value? Life balance experts Lisa Gates and Beth Gordon write that although most of us spend our days chasing our tails, so to speak (or being chased by other people's expectations)—"we all hold a picture in our hearts and minds of what our lives would look like if we were making conscious, integrated, values-based choices."[7]

Imagine what that would look like for you. Really try to picture how it would look. How would the choices you make on a daily basis be different if they were aligned with your values? Gates and Gordon define values this way:

> Simply stated, values are essential, intrinsic qualities of being that inform
> our doings. Values are the building blocks of who we are, and without them
> we're like drifting rudderless dinghies. When we discover (or rediscover)
> what we value most, and make consistent choices that reflect those values,
> all the moving parts or our lives feel congruent and integrated.[8]

This is why it is so important to refine the vision of what you truly want. Without clarity, it is impossible to make values-based choices. Owning your desires is as important as owning your regrets; owning your future is as important as owning your past. When you accept responsibility for changing the things you don't want, you can take responsibility for creating the things you do.

> The very act of accepting responsibility calms your mind and clarifies your vision.
>
> Brian Tracy

---

7. Lisa Gates and Beth Gordon, "How Living in Balance Changes the World: Smaller Steps, Bigger Commitments," *Craving Balance: Purpose Changes Everything*, January 6, 2009, http://www.cravingbalance.com/craving-balance/2009/1/7/how-living-in-balance-changes-the-world-small-steps-bigger-c.html (accessed March 1, 2009).

8. Lisa Gates and Beth Gordon, "What Is Balance?" *Balance Bliss Quickstart*, PDF downloaded March 31, 2009.

⭐ ⭐ ⭐

COACHING MOMENT: SUSAN (CONTINUED)

Remember my client Susan who finally came to terms with her post-baby body? After she defined her problem, it was time for some creative thinking to form an action plan. I helped Susan identify several plans to incorporate more exercise into her life as a busy mom. From those alternatives, she chose to train four times a week in her home gym, which she had never used. She allowed "before" pictures to be taken and hung up. She set five SMART goals (you'll learn about these in chapter five) and agreed to a monthly evaluation to reassess her measurements, weight, cardiovascular endurance, strength, flexibility, and overall wellness.

Susan had become painfully aware that a problem existed regarding her health and appearance. She had analyzed her problem and made a decision to find the root cause. With an evaluation plan set in place, she could stay focused and on task, knowing she would be held accountable for all of her actions.

A problem is just that: a problem. With the proper plan set in place, smart, creative action steps can deliver a wonderful solution.

Recently my husband, Scott, and I were talking about his work and what he really wanted to do with his life and career. It can be tough balancing the need to pay the bills and the need to find work that truly inspires you. I remember telling him, "Listen. Together we can do this. We are a good team. We have overcome quite a few obstacles in the past. Remember when we were trying to move that enormous broken TV that was too heavy for us to lift? We got it off the entertainment center and onto the floor, and then we got a sheet, put it on there, and dragged it across the kitchen and into the garage. Then we stood there and looked at each other because we didn't know what to do next. But then we saw Corbin's skateboard. So we got the TV up on it and rolled it out front and across the parking lot to the Dumpster. If we can do something crazy like that, then getting your career from here to there shouldn't be difficult." We laughed about it, but he agreed. We have been working together ever since as he refines his vision and reaches for his dreams.

Chances are, there is just one little bit of information that can turn your "hopeless" situation into an easy fix. For us, it was spotting the skateboard. What is it for you? All you need are the right tools. But even with the right tools, when you're moving something heavy, you need to work as a team. You can't hope to fix weighty matters at home if you don't work together with your family, and that starts with you and your spouse. If you are not married, it might mean getting the help of your significant other or a close friend. More than likely, if you find something you can support them in, they will be more than willing to support you. It's also likely that you will have to be the one to initiate the conversation. After all, you are the one looking for ways to turn things around. The power is in your hands.

> In the final analysis, the one quality that all successful people have is the ability to take responsibility.
>
> Michael Korda

THE SECRET IS ALREADY INSIDE YOU

It bears repeating that the secrets to your success are already inside you. You just need to do a little excavating.

Certainly you can see things outside you that you want to change. You want to look good, get your home running less frantically, get out of debt or find a better paying job, have more energy to meet all of your obligations, and otherwise get along in the world.

However, those outside, or extrinsic, motivators aren't enough to keep you going long-term. You have to find an *intrinsic,* or internal, source of motivation that works for you alone and has nothing to do with the opinions, values, or expectations of others. In the words of author Barbara Lazear Ascher, "There is a need to discover that we are capable of solitary joy and having experienced it, to know that we have touched the core of self." What at your core gives you, and perhaps only you, this special joy?

I will address extrinsic versus intrinsic motivation in chapter eight, but I want you to know right now that the more you are able to define what motivates you from within, the more motivated you will be over time. You will find meaning and joy in working hard. You will live with greater hope and anticipation because being tuned in to your deepest desires usually means working for the good of something beyond yourself, and working for a higher good will give you an internal satisfaction that a promotion or a paycheck can't provide.

On the other hand, when we are extrinsically motivated, we are working for the approval of those outside ourselves; we are looking for external rewards in the form of recognition or compensation; and, although we are primarily working for the good of our own selves rather than the greater good, we will never achieve lasting internal satisfaction. Instead, those external motivators will let us down, disappoint us, and cause us to expect less over time.

This is not to say that extrinsic motivators are meaningless. In fact, they serve an important purpose in our development. When we are younger, extrinsic motivators teach us the basic mechanics of being responsible. As we mature, however, they become decreasingly meaningful.

It is healthy for a youngster to want to please his or her parents and teachers, be a good citizen, and fit into society. It is part of our socialization that makes us community-minded adults. It is very important to our growth and development to have the encouragement of those close to us and the acceptance of the public at large. In fact, in early development, there is nothing more destructive emotionally than feeling disapproved of or rejected. I still carry the scars of being ostracized by my schoolmates, even though I have long since forgiven them.

I want to challenge you to encourage the young people in your life. We would all do well to remember how important extrinsic motivators are to the well-being of young people. It doesn't take much to let youngsters know they are worth something, that they have gifts and talents the world needs. They need to know there are adults who believe in them. Only when young people are supported by those around them will they be able to look inside and tap into their own intrinsic motivators.

When we exercise our ability to change a young person's life, we bring meaning to our own. This is part of developing character. A person with character steps up to the plate and takes responsibility for what needs to be done for the good of all.

It all begins with refining your vision and being able to respond to whatever life brings you, by courageously *taking* the responsibility for your own dreams and supporting the dreams of others.

You are able. You are fully response-able.

> Between stimulus and response there is a space. In that space is our power to choose our response. In our response lies our growth and our freedom.
>
> Viktor Frankl

RESPONSIBILITY CHALLENGE:
TAKE THE BALL AND RUN WITH IT

Describe the vision you have for your family, marriage, career, personal growth, health, fitness, finances, and even community.

_____

_____

_____

_____

How have you chosen to respond to the discrepancy between your vision and your experience? Rate your *response-ability* when it comes to each of those areas.

_____

_____

_____

_____

Choose your lowest rating and make a plan to close the gap between what you envision and current reality. How will you grab hold of the ball and score the outcome you've dreamed of?

_____

_____

_____

_____

_____

> When you accept full responsibility for a situation, it means you have the power to create the solution.
>
> Debra Moorhead

How you treat yourself today—

right now, at this very moment—

dictates your tomorrow.

CHAPTER 4 ★ ENGAGE YOUR WHOLE SELF

> When you engage in systematic, purposeful action, using and stretching
> your abilities to the maximum, you cannot help but feel positive and
> confident about yourself.
>
> Brian Tracy

When I was younger, I overheard a conversation between my father and his friend. The friend was boasting about something his daughter had done. I heard my dad say, "Boy, I hope someday my daughter makes me proud."

I was young, but I felt the impact and the implications of my father's words. His comment washed over my teen mind like a bucket of cold water. I will never forget that day or those words. They caused me to connect, or engage, deeply with what was happening in my life on an entirely different level. I determined that day to do everything within my power to make my father proud.

This was another defining moment for me. There was no shortage of opportunities for my father to be disappointed in my behavior. Facing this reality forced me to own what kind of a daughter I had been and acknowledge how my actions and attitude affected my dad's impressions and expectations of me. I owned and took responsibility for turning my behavior around. But not only did I take responsibility; I made myself a promise that I would make him proud. I engaged in the process because I had bound myself to it: I made a commitment.

In other words, I engaged my whole self in this pursuit. Engaging is the final step in establishing a strong CORE. We must *choose* to make a change, *own* where we are now, *refine* our vision and take *responsibility* for our dreams, and finally *engage* our whole selves in the process of reaching our dreams.

To *engage* means to fully involve one's self. The word denotes being completely committed to a chosen course of action. Taking *ownership* is looking at your life and deciding what you do and don't want. Taking *responsibility* is acknowledging that "if it is to be, it is up to me." *Engaging*, on the other hand, is committing to see it through.

Being *engaged* is, well, like *being* engaged. It is to wholly devote, involve, enlist, immerse, and enter into. It's like what you do when you pledge to become united with, or agree to marry, another person. The hope is that this union will result in a new whole greater than the sum of your individual lives. Similarly, when you engage with your own potential, you enter into a contract with your own best self to become a whole new you greater than the sum of all of your past experiences.

When you refine your vision and take responsibility for your dreams, you begin setting some quality goals and creating a workable plan. Once you have devised a plan, however, it is time to actively engage in seeing it through. It is time to take action and get things moving.

Ready?

Engage!

> Let him who would move the world first move himself.
>
> Socrates

FROM NOW ON

After the divorce from Jimmy was final, it was time to get back to following my dreams. This was a time of renewed responsibility. Just as on the day I decided I would be a mechanic or a boiler-room tech or a hull repairperson or a hospital corpsman, I decided *from now on* I was responsible for how my life would be. I and no one else.

I was still pretty young, about twenty-one years old, but I determined I would start doing more to make something of myself rather than running after things I wasn't ready to handle. I knew I needed to find something I could be good at, preferably something I could be *the best* at.

I was working in the endoscopy lab at the Oakland Naval Hospital, where we would run those teeny-tiny little cameras or other sensors through the body to do exploratory examinations. I became interested in doing esophageal motility studies (EMS), where a catheter is inserted through the nose and guided into the stomach. As it is being extracted, readings are taken to help diagnose certain disorders in the esophagus (sorry if this is too technical or gross, but it's the kind of thing medical techs do!).

Oddly enough, I really loved this work and was pretty good at it. I pulled together a proposal, presented it to the gastroneurology clinic, and told them, "I would like to run this program for you. I have learned how to do this, and I have researched the results and their values." The department liked my proposal so much that they put me in charge of doing these procedures. I began going into the operating room while they were doing a certain surgery on the lower esophageal sphincter (usually for gastroesophageal reflux disease, GERD), and I would put the esophageal motility probe into the lower esophageal sphincter and measure the pressure as they were doing the surgery.

When I reflect on this time in my life, I realize now that my courage and belief in my abilities developed in the Persian Gulf. It goes to show that we can learn from ourselves, if we let ourselves.

The adventurous experiences and lessons started because we had a lot of downtime during the Gulf War. In addition to my other responsibilities, I was asked to develop a series of in-service trainings for the staff members. To teach the material, I drew on the creative educational techniques I had been exposed to in seventh grade and came up with some fairly unique presentations and educational games. I created board games resembling Candy Land but taught medical terms instead of the names of sweets.

People loved it, and they learned from it. Then I had the class write poetry about different medical procedures to help them understand and memorize the information.

Without realizing it, I was learning how to motivate people by engaging not only their minds but also their hearts. I intuitively knew what media mogul Rupert Murdoch once famously stated: "In motivating people, you've got to engage their minds *and* their hearts." I took this one step further and engaged their bodies too.

It wasn't long before I was teaching exercise classes to keep the staff at my commands healthy and fit. I continued through each transfer as well. Taking the initiative and stepping up as a leader and trainer challenged me to continually improve my techniques. Soon I was winning awards and earning commendations for my work ethic and performance. Wherever I was, I wanted to help people grow and become better at what they did. I was tapping into my passions and learning from myself, which laid the foundation for me to overcome challenges way back then and still today.

When I realized these strengths in myself, I began to focus and empower myself to move forward. I learned how to master a craft, to present what I knew to others, to exemplify the confidence that would instill trust in them, and to embrace success. As a result, I was able to take step after step forward. I found myself working alongside doctors in the operating room because I had refined my vision, taken responsibility, and fully engaged myself in developing a specific expertise. I had found a craft and mastered it, and this propelled me forward time and time again.

> I will study and get ready, and perhaps my chance will come.
>
> Abraham Lincoln

MIND YOUR P'S AND HEED YOUR CUES

I don't do esophageal motility studies anymore, but I do still teach and train. Just because you find something you do well doesn't mean you'll do it for the rest of your life, but you can take what you learn into your next phase of life. I still create new techniques, come up with innovative teaching ideas, develop new presentations and curricula, and talk to people about being their best. All of these things began with those studies. Everything I did as a hospital corpsman still helps me today, even what I learned about proper bedside manner.

I'll bet along the way you've already learned the skills you need to fulfill your dreams. If you look back at everything you've been through, you will be surprised how your life experiences have equipped you to become who you've always dreamed of becoming. Don't take those experiences for granted.

But even when you think you've got it all figured out, never, never, never stop learning. Engage your whole self in the process of learning. I am always looking for ways to improve my game and get to the next level. If I'm not engaged in the process of reaching higher, how can I help others reach higher? There is a very real high that comes from learning and giving when you know it emanates from what motivates you deep within.

When you have this kind of motivation, this is when engagement is so important. It continues to propel you forward. When you're engaged, whatever you do, you'll do it to the best of your ability. And whenever you feel you are doing your best, you'll push yourself to do even better.

Most people are simply afraid to engage because they're indecisive. For example, many kids entering college are told, "It's okay to go to school and declare your major as *undecided*." What's with that? Choosing anything is better than choosing nothing. Whether in college or in life, you can always change your mind, but choose something and commit to learning all you can about it. Hook up your internal motivators to get yourself excited about something—anything. Engage, determined to excel at whatever it is. Even if you change your direction in a few months, at least you have added a specific area of study to your knowledge base. On the other hand, if you continually wander through life not aiming at anything in particular, you will be surprisingly disappointed at where you end up.

After leaving Oakland Navy Hospital, I grabbed my next assignment with both hands. I was reassigned to the *Emory S. Land*, a sub tender, a ship that goes out to supply and service submarines at sea, whose homeport was in Norfolk, Virginia. I lived onshore and went to work on the ship every day.

In peacetime, naval ships can still be dangerous places because they are constantly running drills to maintain standards of readiness in case they're ever called into duty. With roughly fifteen hundred sailors on board, that meant the medics had no shortage of small accidents to tend to. Being the only surgical tech on board, I was given the opportunity to handle a lot of the smaller accidents by myself—sewing stitches and so forth. As members of the crew, medics also had to help maintain the ship and train to be ready in case of emergencies. In addition to being an EMT, I was trained to fight fires and treat injuries remotely when people couldn't make it to medical. I was also part of an emergency response medical team called the Flying Squad. Not only did we get to wear extremely cool outfits (what better reason to sign on?), but whenever there was a call to be on the helicopter landing deck, all of the other crew members had to get out of my way as I ran through the corridors. (That was pretty cool, too!)

Looking back, I realize this was a pivotal point in my life. During one general quarters drill there was a need for someone to do stretcher bearer and first aid training on the flight deck. Since I was the only corpsman available at the time, they sent me. I would shout an instruction and then yell, "What did I just say?" and have them repeat it. I was empowering them and myself at the same time. Next thing you know, I was responsible for all of the medical damage control qualifications. I then became the affiliate faculty member for the basic life support program, training everybody and also training people to be CPR instructors themselves.

Everyone had to learn a significant amount of information about everyone else's department, and I was overseeing every aspect of the cross-training. I created this big, one-woman show. They liked it so much that they would have me go out and do medical training at other commands. As a result, I went to school to get my master trainer instructor certificate through the military, started teaching at the Great Lakes Naval Hospital Corps School, and was launched into public speaking.

After Norfolk, I was stationed in the Hospital Corps School in the Great Lakes area. I spent my time there teaching recruits to be medics and to do nursing procedures, practice emergency medicine, and perform all the basic fundamentals of hospital corpsman work. Everything was going so well, and I was fully engaged in reaching my goals. Just before my last transfer, however, I faced one of the worst setbacks of my life.

My father, whom I was so determined to make proud, had a heart attack and died. I literally left Norfolk, went to his bedside, and suctioned his mouth as life support was turned off. Just as quickly, I had to leave to go to the Great Lakes area. Dad's death broke my heart, but it was especially tough for me because of the events leading up to it.

Dad was scheduled for a routine surgery. I had considered flying in for the surgery, but I planned to wait and visit him over Father's Day right after the surgery while he was recovering. Had I gone to be with him for the surgery, however, I would have been in the house the night before he went into the hospital, the night he had the heart attack. I found out later from his doctor that if someone had been there who knew CPR, he probably would have survived. It was a devastating revelation for me.

All of my life I had been working to make my dad proud, and he died because no one was there who knew CPR. In the meantime, I was training people to perform CPR and other emergency procedures. It was a horrible trick of fate. I could have made a difference. Even though I was trained and ready, I was in the wrong place at the wrong time. I couldn't help the man I loved the most in life.

I've had to learn to forgive myself, but at the same time it is hard not to wonder *What if?* and feel the pain that my father never knew his grandchildren because he passed away before they were ever born.

The cure for grief is motion.

Elbert Hubbard

Don't Let Chance Derail Your Destiny

Looking back, I realize I would much rather have known what was needed to save my dad's life and not have been there than to have been there and not been trained in CPR. While I missed that opportunity to help save a life, there were many other lives I was able to help while serving as a medic.

Fate will throw us some tests we will inevitably fail, but it is the overall journey, not each setback, that matters. When you are fully engaged in pursuing your destiny, you can't afford to let circumstance disengage you. There will be some twists and turns and retracing of steps along the way, but I can tell you it is worth sticking with it and following through on your dreams.

I used to be a cheerleader, but I am not a cheerleader today. I went to modeling school, but I am not a full-time model. I am a trained EMT, but I am not a practicing medic. Though I didn't stay with those things, I did learn from them and am better for what I know of them today. Because I engaged with what was before me, I have grown and have more talents than I would have had otherwise, and all of this has come from the decision to not let life happen to me but to go out and happen to life. I determined to make the most of every opportunity in order to make the most of me so I could make the greatest difference. Every activity and learning opportunity I have engaged in has contributed something valuable to make me who I am now.

Engagement is not about going through life passively. It's about making decisions for yourself and choosing a path wholeheartedly, even if that path is not the one you are ultimately destined to walk. I can guarantee, though, that this path will have something to do with bringing you closer to your ultimate destination. When you are fully engaged in the process of becoming your best self, you will find you are continually reevaluating and asking yourself what you should be learning from your present situation. You will have to continually make adjustments.

This is what balance is all about. Have you ever stood on one foot and wobbled back and forth? Making continual, little adjustments is how you maintain your balance, and you'll notice all of those little adjustments your body is forced to make to stay balanced will engage your core. Nothing strengthens your core like trying to maintain your balance in a precarious position. The more you engage, the stronger you become.

Life balance coaches Lisa Gates and Beth Gordon teach that engagement and balance go hand in hand. When we are fully engaged, we are able to see the bigger picture and invest ourselves in what truly matters to us.

> If our goals are set and achieved, if our life is in balance and humming
> along, we are engaged. We get invested in the solutions to the problems
> that plague our hearts. We rescue dogs, we feed starving children, we
> run for public office, we heal our relationships and shake hands with
> our enemies. We change the world.[9]

When you're engaged, you look at the path before you and say, "Here are my action steps. I don't care how old I am. This is what I will do, and after I do it, I will tell someone younger than me that they can do it, too."

Everybody wants to make a difference—to influence the world and leave a legacy. But we don't just arrive at the end of the line and then discover we have done worthwhile things. Engaging each and every day is what gets us where we ultimately want to be.

It's about getting up each morning and choosing to do what it takes to achieve your goals. What you failed at yesterday and what you plan to do tomorrow don't count. It's all about what you do today.

> Don't wait for extraordinary opportunities. Seize common occasions and
> make them great.
>
> Orison Swett Marden

TO ENGAGE OR DISENGAGE

From the day I walked into the military, I began mapping my journey. I served for

---

9. Lisa Gates, "What's the Ultimate Benefit of Setting Goals and Getting in Balance?" *Craving Balance: Purpose Changes Everything*, February 27, 2009, http:// www.cravingbalance.com/craving-balance/2009/2/27/whats-the-ultimate-benefit-of-setting-goals-and-getting-in-b.html (accessed March 1, 2009).

twelve years—and they were twelve years of engagement for me. In some ways they were the toughest of my life, but they were also some of the best. They showed me I could succeed at anything I set my mind to. Not many people have a résumé with a list as long as mine related to health and wellness. Looking back, I recognize that everything I have done since the time I stepped into the military has prepared me for what I am doing in the present moment as a personal trainer, wellness coach, speaker, and author.

For many people, the military offers an incredibly rewarding career path wherein they continue to grow in their chosen fields. For me, I was faced with a decision at this particular juncture. I had the chance to go to Hawaii as my next port of duty. I had to weigh my options.

I felt that continuing on to Hawaii would be disengaging for me; it would take me further away from my purpose. I knew I would likely be "promoted" to some administrative position, and deep down I knew an office job would not give me the access I needed to help people the way I was built to.

It was a fork in the road, and I had to take the best path for me, even if it was the one less traveled. I made that choice. I decided to leave the Navy and start the next phase of my life. Had I decided to be a career military person, I would have ended up as a secretary instead of a wellness coach. I'm glad I stayed fully engaged.

At every crossroads, we need to ask ourselves about the paths ahead and consider which one will keep us best engaged and which will disengage us. What will you do to stay engaged?

> How much do you engage yourself in what's truly real and important in life? That's the individual question.
>
> Ted Danson

LEAVE A LASTING IMPRESSION

While I miss my dad, I remember and honor him best by living the way he taught me to live. My dad was really big on quality of life. Later in his life he became a recruiter and owned a franchise of management recruiters. The last thing he told me the final time I saw him alive was that he had finally "made it." He had finally plugged into his dream. His life's goal was to be able to take people out of dead-end jobs and help them find fulfilling opportunities where they could be what they wanted to be.

In this way, I am most certainly my father's daughter. He was a great speaker and always very charismatic and magnetic. People were drawn to him. He was all about trying to help as many people as he could. I am probably more like him than I realized most of my life. In the last few years, I have seen part of his spirit ingrained in me. A parent will always have a lasting effect on a child, sometimes without even knowing it. He has been gone for a long time now, but a big part of who I am today is a result of what he showed me about himself while I was still a kid.

What impression are you leaving? How are you engaging in the people and things that matter most?

> Are you in earnest? Seize this very minute. Boldness has genius, power, and magic in it. Only engage, and then the mind grows heated. Begin, and then the work will be completed.
>
> Jean Anouilh

STEP IT UP!

Do something you've never done before. For example, enter a triathlon. Here are eight helpful tips to help you go about it:

1   Find an event and register for it.

2   Remember: Walking is an option.

3   Find a group to train with. Consider joining a spin class to get you started.

4   Find a friend or two to ride or run with on the weekends.

5   When you start to say, "I can't," or "I won't be able to because—," stop. Look at yourself and say, "But I can try."

6   Remember: Consistency is key. Make a plan and stick to it. It will help if you have a friend or a group to hold you accountable.

7   Set clear goals for each training session. For example, ride five miles this week; next week, ride ten. Incorporate related training, such as a group swim or interval training into your week.

8   Create a reward system. Get your whole group involved. Look forward to the rewards and talk about them often during training. Dangle those precious rewards like carrots. Sounds funny, but it works.

PART TWO

STRENGTH to See It Through

YOU ARE SMARTER AND STRONGER THAN YOU KNOW.

THE POWER OF EIGHT

In every phenomenon the beginning remains always the most notable moment.

Thomas Carlyle

As we begin this next section, I want to stop for a moment and talk about the number eight. Why? Well, because the number eight is sort of a theme going forward. The next section is all about the eight in *Motiv8n'*, the eight core tips for fitness represented by the eight letters in the word STRENGTH. This is also where I introduce eight guest experts who will coach you in the eight key areas of overall life fitness.

Why do I think the number eight is so great (other than being a fun way to spell *Motiv8n'*)? For starters, numerologists define the number eight as the number of power. Many esoteric traditions teach that the number eight represents the attainment of balance. In other traditions, eight is the number of accomplishment and achievement.[10] The word for *eight* in Chinese is similar to the word for *wealth* or *fortune*. Laid on its side, it is the symbol for infinity, "the constant flow of energy, perpetual motion, and the continuance of life."[11] In biblical numerology, it is the number of new beginnings—and that's the thing I like most about the number eight.

My philosophy of motivation is all about new beginnings. Each new day presents a new opportunity to grow stronger. Every day you choose to get up and do your push-ups, every decision you make to eat clean foods, every time you take a step toward achieving a goal—each of these represents the chance at a new start. It motivates me to know that every moment is a chance to get closer to becoming the best I can be. How about you?

10. Lynn Hayes, "The Power of Eight," *Beliefnet*, August 5, 2008. http://blog.beliefnet.com/astrologicalmusings/2008/08/the-power-of-eight.html (accessed May 1, 2009).

11. Christine Delorey, "The Power of Eight," *Creative Numerology*, July 26, 2008. http://creativenumerology.wordpress.com/2008/07/26/the-power-of-eight/ (accessed May 1, 2009).

The great Oliver Wendell Holmes once said, "The great thing in this world is not so much where we are, as in what direction we are moving." Abraham Lincoln said it this way: "A goal properly set is halfway reached." Ausonius counseled, "Begin—to begin is half the work, let half still remain; again begin this, and thou wilt have finished." The Roman poet Horace penned, "He has the deed half done who has made a beginning." Oh, but don't forget it was Plato who wrote, "The beginning is the most important part of the work."

It's all about beginnings. How do you begin well? You start by implementing the eight action steps outlined in the next section. The operative word here is *start*, as in simply taking action. We don't want to take just *any* action, however. We want to take the *right* action. We want to take actions aligned with our true motives.

Motivation is made up of two parts. The first part is *motive.* We've spent some time addressing motives, and we'll dig into them more deeply still in Part Two. The second part is *-ation.* As a rule, this suffix takes the noun and turns it into an "action or process: something connected with an action or process."[12] How will you act on your motives? By building STRENGTH to see them through. In the chapters ahead, you'll learn eight core tips to build that STRENGTH: setting SMART goals, thinking about what you want, revving up your relationships, empowering yourself, negating the negatives, giving back with gratitude, taking charge, and harnessing the power of humility, honesty, and humor. That's the power of eight in *Motiv8n'.* It is taking your inner convictions and turning them into outward successes. It's the power to demonstrate your strength by knowing what you want and aligning every action with that desire.

At the end of each of the next eight chapters, I will help you establish life fitness goals and achieve greater strength in eight fundamental areas:

1   Financial Fitness

2   Functional Fitness (Organization)

3   Friends and Family Fitness (Relationships)

4   Focused Fitness (Vocation)

5   Feeling Fitness (Emotions)

---

12. *Merriam-Webster Online Dictionary,* s.v. "-ation," http://www.merriam-webster.com/dictionary/-ation (accessed May 1, 2009).

6 Witness the Fitness (Spirituality, Gratitude)

7 Feeding Your Fitness (Nutrition)

8 Funny Bone Fitness (Humility, Honesty, Humor)

These eight areas are the building blocks to a balanced, whole, and healthy life. Failing in any one of these areas can derail your best fitness intentions in any other area. For example, when your finances or relationships are a mess, your emotions get all out of whack. When you're stressed or sad, you set yourself up to make unhealthy food choices. Poor food choices sap your strength and energy, which further demotivates you from exercising or from making any self-improvement effort at all. You lose sight of your dreams to do great things and be a positive force in the world. You can even start feeling increasingly bitter as you begin feeling decreasingly grateful for the good things you *do* have. The next thing you know, you're caught in a downward spiral of feeling weak and out of control.

To maximize your motivational STRENGTH, you need to maintain a strong and balanced life. When you do, you will have the capability, confidence, and courage to consistently choose your best future.

The key to beginning well is beginning with the end in mind. William James said, "It is our attitude at the beginning of a difficult task which, more than anything else, will affect its successful outcome." Hopefully, by now, you have adjusted some mindsets or reevaluated some self-perceptions and are ready to forge on with a clearer head and a more expectant heart.

It's time to saddle up and ride into *your* new beginning.

> The future is always beginning now.
>
> Mark Strand

Break it down;

then break it down again.

*Break it into teeny bites
that almost melt
in your mouth.*

SET SMART GOALS

> It does not take much strength to do things, but it requires great strength to decide on what to do.
>
> Elbert Hubbard

Goals are amazing things. Look back at what you've accomplished when you had a clear goal in front of you. When you wanted to get on the football team or the cheerleading squad or into college or when you wanted that job or promotion, you did what it took to make it happen.

Now think about those times when you didn't have a particular goal in front of you, and look at what you achieved. Um, what was it you achieved? Probably nothing. To develop motivational STRENGTH and accomplish great things, the first action step you must take is to set SMART goals.

People rarely accomplish anything great without a goal. Nor do they suddenly fall into a fitness routine if they haven't set a measurable goal to get in shape or lose weight. No one grows stronger or improves in any area without the motivation that goals provide. Goals are what propel us forward. The smarter the goal, the further you'll go.

Only 3 percent of the U.S. population practices any kind of goal setting. What's shocking is that this same 3 percent accomplish more than the other 97 percent combined. When you hear that 85 percent of all of the world's wealth is held by 10 percent of the world's population, it makes you wonder if among that 10 percent are the 3 percent who set goals.

The interesting thing about a goal is how effective it is in getting a person to reach increasingly greater heights. The human brain is wired to actively pursue challenging goals. Once it formulates an intellectually believable goal and commits to it emotionally, it drives toward it with an irresistible energy.

Success guru Max Steingart states: "Reality forms around your commitments. The achievement of your goal is assured the moment you commit yourself to it." At the turn of the century, early American writer Elbert Hubbard wrote, "Many people fail in life, not for lack of ability or brains or even courage, but simply because they have never organized their energies around a goal."

The key to motivation is focusing your energy, and the way you do that is by organizing all of the different types of energy emerging from your consciousness around a specific, measurable, time-sensitive goal. Andrew J. DuBrin wrote the textbook for a class I took on behavioral psychology, and this is what he had to say about the stimulating power of a challenging goal in his book *Getting It Done*: "Setting difficult and specific goals improves performance. Goal setting is therefore as important to the self-disciplined achiever as an engine is to a vehicle." He further explains how the body responds to goal setting:

> Another interesting scientific fact about goals is that they have an arousal effect on the brain. When you establish challenging goals, your heart rate increases, and as the heart rate increases, you become more mentally aroused or energized to reach the goal. The arousal appears to be related to setting higher goals. . . . Setting goals thus becomes a self-feeding cycle.[13]

Goals are what keep us energized and moving in the right direction. They are beacons that guide our course when other forces threaten to pull us aside. In *The War of Art*, author Steven Pressfield identifies all such forces as *Resistance*. He states, "Resistance is the most toxic force on the planet. . . . To yield to Resistance deforms our spirit. It stunts us and makes us less than we are and were born to be."[14]

Goals are what provide the empowering motivation to overcome resistance; they

---

13. This and the preceding quotation are from Andrew J. DuBrin, *Getting It Done: The Transforming Power of Self-Discipline* (New Jersey: Princeton's/Pacesetter Books, 1995), 23.
14. Steven Pressfield, *The War of Art: Break Through the Blocks and Win Your Inner Creative Battles* (New York: Grand Central Publishing, 2002), Preface.

are the North Star pointing us toward our destination even as the ever-present tides and currents of daily distractions threaten to ground us. This is how parenting expert Fitzhugh Dodson explains it: "Without goals, and plans to reach them, you are like a ship that has set sail with no destination."

> Progress has little to do with speed, but much to do with direction.
>
> Author Unknown

ANCHORS AWAY

The last year I was in the Navy, still mourning my father's death, I was a bit directionless. Returning to the Great Lakes after my father passed away, I suppose I had "set sail with no destination." I was hurting and a little lost in transition. I longed for stability and someone to fill the emptiness in my heart from losing my dad and leaving everything familiar behind. In search, I fell in love with a very charismatic, charming, and romantic man. Six months later, we were married. A year later, I gave birth to Corbin. Six months after, I was a newly divorced single mother looking for work.

I can't say I regret any of it, because I was blessed with the gift of Corbin. I will never forget how I felt when I first met Corbin's dad, Rolf. He totally swept me off my feet.

Rolf's father was the famous Dieter Dengler, who escaped from a POW camp in Laos during the Vietnam War. A movie was made about him called *Rescue Dawn*, starring Christian Bale as Dieter. In 2001, when Corbin was about two, Dieter died of Lou Gehrig's disease. At the time my son was his only grandson, and after he passed away, FOX News came to our house to interview us. In 2007, when the movie premiered, Christian Bale invited Corbin and Rolf to come to New York and spend the week. This was a golden opportunity for my son, and as he's grown up, he has continued to have some amazing experiences with his dad.

Nevertheless, things did get a little rough after the divorce. I was a new single mom, new to the civilian workplace, and now a new homeowner. I so desperately wanted to provide a stable home for my son that I bought a house. Having just left the Navy, I took any job I could get, not considering the cost of commuting, insurance, day care, mortgage, and so on. I was used to having my living expenses paid for. Even though what I took home in the Navy seemed negligible compared to my new salary, I didn't calculate the cost of living against my new income. I got behind on everything, and the house was foreclosed on a year after I bought it.

The series of events leading to the foreclosure actually began the day after my father's heart attack, when I was still stationed in Virginia. My father lay in a coma as I drove to the airport to catch a flight to see him. I was heading down a six-lane highway when a car going the opposite direction did a U-turn across three lanes of traffic, pulling into the middle lane in front of me. Instead of speeding up with traffic, the driver braked. I slammed into the back of the car. The car was totaled by my SUV, but miraculously nobody was hurt, including the three people who emerged from the car, not even wearing any shoes. I explained what happened to the police officer, but he issued both of us traffic violations. The woman was ticketed for driving without a driver's license, and I got a ticket for running into her. The officer explained if I went to court my ticket would be dismissed since I was not at fault. I did go and was completely cleared by the judge of any fault for this accident.

Well, the story doesn't end there. The other party hired a lawyer, sued me, and served the lawsuit papers to my Virginia address, only I wasn't there because I had been transferred to the Hospital Corps School in the Great Lakes area. I was forced to hire a lawyer with money I didn't have. I spent five thousand dollars on fees, phone calls, and airfare because by the time all of this unraveled I had already been married and divorced. Yet after all of the time, expense, and emotional energy I invested, they still served a final notice for me to appear in court at the old Virginia address, knowing full well I now lived in Chicago. Because I failed to appear, I lost the suit and was ordered to pay their claim of forty-five thousand dollars.

By now my house had gone into foreclosure because I couldn't afford to pay the mortgage. I was paying seven hundred dollars per month for day care, driving eighty miles each way to work, and paying for a defense lawyer. I didn't know what to do. I was still kind of young, about twenty-eight, and I didn't know how to make it all work as a single mom not able to make ends meet, losing my house, and being sued for more money than I earned in a year. It was also my first year out of the military. I had made the mistake of not calculating the actual cost of living, including childcare *and* day care, compared to the money I was actually bringing home. I was doing far worse than if I'd stayed in the service but wasn't smart enough to realize it back then.

I had no idea what to do, so I filed for bankruptcy. It was a horrible and humiliating experience. But I was learning valuable lessons, and I had places to go.

> Sometimes the path you're on is not as important as the direction you're heading.
>
> Kevin Smith

WHAT DOESN'T KILL YOU MAKES YOU STRONGER

My first job out of the service, as you might guess, was as a health educator for Blue Cross Blue Shield. I created an awesome stress management class using stories from my extremely stressful life as a basis for the lessons. I started learning about motivation theory simply because it's what helped keep me from feeling completely overcome by my own circumstances. I was trying to motivate myself as much as I was anyone else.

This was right before I filed for bankruptcy, right before I got out of the house and moved closer to work. One evening, while sitting in a six-hour traffic jam during a terrible snowstorm with Corbin crying in the backseat, I was racking my brain, thinking, *What is going on? Why is all of this happening?* And then I came up with this life-defining statement, which turned my whole perspective around: "My strength is defined not by the absence of moments of weakness but by my ability to overcome in them."

I realized if I was going to grow stronger and turn things around, I would have to set some smarter goals. It wasn't that I hadn't set goals before; it was just that I hadn't set well-defined goals. My goals a year earlier had been to find stability for Corbin and me, to find a job, buy a house, and provide a stable environment for my son. I just wanted to plant our lives somewhere and not have to be moving around all of the time. I had sent out a thousand résumés and applied for countless jobs until I had found something—anything.

I had set three main goals: buy a house, get a job, and find day care—and that's what I'd done, in that order. The problem wasn't that my goals were necessarily bad, or even too lofty, but I didn't divide each one down into doable steps. I should have broken each goal apart to make sure it was realistic and attainable and the methods I used to pursue it would actually help me accomplish it. Had I looked at these things first, then *maybe* I wouldn't have ended up taking a job that didn't pay enough money to provide for my child and myself or that was eighty miles from my home—which is how I ended up filing bankruptcy and foreclosing on my house.

I learned from experience that setting SMART goals was the key to avoiding the stress caused by *not* having set them. I wouldn't be a victim of my own lack of planning ever again—or so I thought!

Are you engaged in the process of reaching your goals? You have to wrap your mind around what you intend to see happen exactly, establish some clear expectations, work out every detail, and continually reevaluate where you're headed. You have to keep your life in check and know how you will balance all of your priorities going forward. I know so many people who have great jobs and make tons of money but their home lives are in shambles. I know people who are respected leaders in their communities but whose marriages are failing, and I know others who are passionately pursuing their dreams but not making enough money to pay the bills. You have to set specific goals in *every* area of your life and make sure they are all moving together in the same direction.

I won't pretend I learned my lesson when it comes to financial planning, because to this day I still have my share of money troubles. In fact, there were more lessons I had to learn about investing in property, but I've saved that for another chapter. But I did learn that each of us needs to map things out ahead of time. Even though we can't plan for the bumps, we can still do some navigating. My lack of planning put me behind the power curve, so when I did hit a bump I lost everything.

Be ready. Just because you have things together doesn't mean something bad can't happen to you and the rug can't suddenly be yanked out from under your feet. You have to decide now, before it ever happens, that you will bounce back, learn from your mistakes, and set new goals.

That's what I did, and here I am today as living proof that rebounding from the bleakest of circumstances is *always* possible.

> The best opportunities in life are the ones we create. Goal setting provides for you the opportunity to create an extraordinary life.
>
> Gary Ryan Blair

WHAT IS A SMART GOAL?

The first thing I do when I begin working with a client is to teach him or her to set SMART goals in every area of life. Although most clients come to me with a weight loss goal, I initially have them set one goal in each of the eight fitness areas: finances, organization, relationships, vocation, emotions, spiritual wellness, nutrition, and humor.

Even though my client's overall goal might be to lose twenty pounds, her SMART goals will have more to do with the incremental healthy steps she plans to take in each of the other areas of life. George T. Doran first used the now-widely known term "S.M.A.R.T. goal" in 1981 in a *Management Review* article titled "There's a S.M.A.R.T. Way to Write Management Goals and Objectives." SMART goals have to do with daily choices, where the rubber meets the road, when it comes to planning, organization, and that dreaded word *self-discipline*. Everything else we do to improve and grow stronger is built on the foundation of sound goals. Without having set SMART goals, there will be no long-term growth in any area, especially your health and wellness.

When I come alongside clients to help them achieve their weight loss goals, I see it as an opportunity to help them change their lives and the lives of everyone around them. I grasp the chance to help them maximize their potential and fulfill their lifelong dreams, whatever those might be. It is my hope that stronger, healthier, happier people will make the world a stronger, healthier, happier place. My goal is to help them stay on the path toward their goals.

There's nothing worse than good intentions being derailed by poor planning. Unfulfilled expectations only feed feelings of discouragement and despair, which don't contribute to the world's health and happiness. I don't want you to experience another false start or only temporary success. I want you to get on the road to strength and personal victory *for good*. Living smart means planning smart, and that requires SMART goals.

For a goal to be SMART, it needs to have all of the following characteristics:

1. SPECIFIC
2. MEASURABLE
3. ATTAINABLE
4. REALISTIC
5. TIME-BOUND

Let's briefly run through each of these.

A SMART GOAL IS SPECIFIC

A SMART goal must first be *specific*. Just because you've specified a goal doesn't make it specific. Specific goals actually outline the incremental steps you will take to accomplish your *overall* goal, which might be something like getting in shape. For example, if your general goal is to lose weight, clarifying *what* and *how* you'll do it would be your specific goal. A goal of exercising one hour three times per week is a specific goal you can *do*, while losing twenty pounds is a general goal that merely describes the desired outcome—the destination but not the mode of transportation.

Once you have a destination in mind, you need to get out a map, plot your course, and decide what would be the best vehicle to get you there. The more specific it is, the better. You can start by asking yourself some questions: *What kind of exercise should I do? Where should I exercise? When? For how long? With whom?*

> I feel that the most important step in any major accomplishment is setting a specific goal. This enables you to keep your mind focused on your goal and off the many obstacles that will arise when you're striving to do your best.
>
> Kurt Thomas

A SMART GOAL IS MEASURABLE

Second, a SMART goal must be *measurable.* How will you measure your progress? When your goal is measurable, you are able to stay on track, reach targets and set new ones, and experience the thrill of accomplishment, which will spur you on toward more achievements. Measurable goals help you gain momentum as you mark your progress and see improvement. A measurable goal might include, for example, how much time or how many miles you'll run, how many reps you'll do with which weight, or at what point you'll know you need to raise the bar.

> Those who are successful are those who have more realistic goals. Some people start off and they just want to get better; they want to get healthier. It's not measurable. Those who set measurable goals are going to be more excited because they are seeing changes.
>
> Steve Kaczmarski

A SMART GOAL IS ATTAINABLE

Third, a SMART goal must be *attainable*. When you identify goals that are important to you, you will begin to explore ways to attain them. You'll figure out the skills and resources—information, training, or support—required to make it happen. When you believe your goal is attainable, it will affect your mind-set. You will start to see new opportunities you didn't notice before. Goals that before seemed out of reach will appear to move closer. Personal achievement expert Gene Donohue explains that this is "not because your goals shrink, but because you grow and expand to match them." He adds, "When you list your goals you build your self-image. You see yourself as worthy of these goals, and develop the traits and personality that allow you to possess them."

> The most important thing when learning how to set goals is to clearly see what you're after. Put your inner desires into achievable goals; take action on those goals and you will be successful.
>
> Mike Brescia

A SMART GOAL IS REALISTIC

Fourth, a SMART goal must be *realistic*. A realistic goal must represent an objective toward which you are both willing and able to work. It needs to be both challenging and realistic in order to motivate you; only you can know what that balance is. "A high goal is frequently easier to reach than a low one because a low goal exerts low motivational force," Gene Donohue has stated.

Former UCLA basketball coach John Wooden asserts, "Difficult yet realistic goals produce purpose-directed lives." Goals give your life purpose. Furthermore, the more purposeful you are, the more goal-oriented you will become.

To know whether a goal is realistic, ask yourself if you have ever achieved anything similar in the past or what conditions need to be in place for you to accomplish such a goal. As long as you wholeheartedly believe you can accomplish a goal you set, it is realistic for you.

> Part of the issue of achievement is to be able to set realistic goals, but that's one of the hardest things to do because you don't always know exactly where you're going—and you shouldn't.
>
> George Lucas

A SMART GOAL IS **TIME-BOUND**

Finally, a SMART goal must be *time-bound*. A goal needs to be set within a certain frame of time. If there are no time boundaries, there will be no impetus to complete the goal by a definable future moment. A goal without a deadline is just a dream, but if you take that dream and give it a deadline, then you have a goal.

If you dream of exercising but don't tie any time frame to that dream, it will probably never happen. Give yourself a deadline (no more than thirty days), and it'll become a SMART goal you can attain. "Someday goals" never seem to make it into the present; they always remain out there floating around somewhere in the future. On the other hand, if you anchor every goal with a deadline, then you've automatically set your unconscious mind into motion toward completing it *in the present*. That's one of the most powerful things you can do.

> Crystallize your goals. Make a plan for achieving them and set yourself a deadline. Then, with supreme confidence, determination, and disregard for obstacles and other people's criticisms, carry out your plan.
>
> Paul Meyer

GOALS, ROLES, AND LIFE BALANCE

To make sure the goals you set in one area of your life are especially SMART, you will need to balance them with the goals you set in every other area. If you focus all of your energy on achieving only your career goals, for example, it won't be long before you realize your life is out of balance because your family relationships and your health are suffering. When your *life* is out of balance, your health and wellness will be out of balance, too. So in the pages ahead, keep the eight areas of overall fitness (financial, organizational, relational, vocational, emotional, spiritual, nutritional, and "funny bone" fitness) in mind as you set your goals.

In my experience as a life coach and fitness trainer, I've noticed that ordinary folks have extraordinary difficulty controlling their weight when they are feeling out of control in other areas of their lives. Maybe if you're a competitive bodybuilder or professional athlete you can keep up the momentum for your fitness while the creditors are knocking at your door—but for most of us, when our finances are falling apart, the first thing we let go is our motivation to eat clean and exercise every day. (I know because it's happened to me.)

The same is true for each area of fitness. When we are weak in one area, weakness saps our strength and demotivates us in every area. If you want to grow stronger for life, you have to begin by strengthening your *whole* life.

Researchers have found that men and women approach the process of goal setting and life balance differently. These inherent differences will affect each person's ability to successfully set SMART goals.

What research shows is that men tend to compartmentalize their lives into neat little boxes and, if they can help it, none of those boxes will ever touch or spill their contents into any of the other boxes. Work is kept separate from home, as is hanging out with the guys, fishing, taking care of the car, or watching football. You will probably get a confused, blank stare from your husband, for instance, if in the middle of a football game you ask him a question about his job. With this in mind, you can see how men are more likely to have goals arranged in neat categories that don't necessarily intersect.

Women, on the other hand, tend to store everything in the same laundry basket they carry around with them everywhere they go. The nice thing about this is that nothing in their lives is too far from anything else, and their goals have a way of affecting more than one area at once. Getting in shape, for instance, isn't just about looking good but about finding the energy to make it through the day. Looking great and feeling good might give a woman more pep at work, and healthy eating and exercise habits affect how she raises her kids. As a result, the way a woman leaves the house is often the way she enters the office. Her to-do list has as much to do with the client she needs to call during her commute as it does with the items she needs to pick up for dinner on the way home.

Because of these differences in men and women, each of us will need to approach goal setting in different ways to ensure balance in every area of life. For men, it will likely mean purposefully setting goals in four or five different areas. For women, it might mean setting goals to reflect things we want to accomplish that touch as many parts of our lives as possible.

A tool commonly used to help people understand how to balance the different areas of life is called a Life Wheel. I've modified this tool by creating an octagon with each side representing one of the eight fitness areas we will be working on throughout the rest of this book. Each of these areas is dependent upon the other. For example, all of these areas combined will ultimately determine your physical fitness success. To begin, I would like you to rate your level of satisfaction in each area on a scale from one to eight (with eight being the most satisfied; eight is represented by the outer limit of the wheel, and one is at the center). Again, the eight fitness areas are as follows:

1 Financial Fitness

2 Functional Fitness (Organization)

3 Friends and Family Fitness (Relationships)

4 Focused Fitness (Vocation)

5 Feeling Fitness (Emotions)

6 Witness the Fitness (Spirituality, Gratitude)

7 Feeding Your Fitness (Nutrition)

8 Funny Bone Fitness (Humility, Honesty, Humor)

You might end up with something that looks like this crazy-looking spiderweb. The goal is to achieve overall fitness by focusing on each of these areas. The more balance you have among these eight areas, the more fit your whole life will be. I've included a blank Life Wheel in the Appendix for you to fill out.

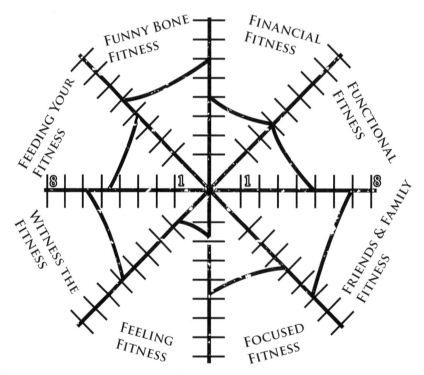

This gives you a bird's-eye view of the areas you already feel good about and which need more attention so that you can have more balance in your life. You will be setting goals in all eight areas as you go, and some will be more challenging than others. But there is no need to feel overwhelmed. As you continue to read, you will work through each one of these areas separately to analyze what you want to accomplish and break it down into bite-sized pieces.

> You don't have to be a fantastic hero to do certain things. . . . You can be just an ordinary chap, sufficiently motivated to reach challenging goals.
>
> Edmund Hillary

MOTIV8N' SAM

Let me introduce you to Sam. Sam is the thirtysomething operations director of special events at Medallion Press. He agreed to work with me because he wanted to lose eighty pounds—or so he thought. At our initial meeting, we talked about his frustration with losing weight, but it wasn't long before we were talking about some of the other areas where he was feeling frustrated. As I got to know Sam, I learned he was also struggling with issues regarding his financial future. He hadn't saved for retirement and had no money in savings, no working budget, and no life insurance. Financial frustrations, I believe, created a sense of uncertainty, which was at the center of his weight problem. Lack of financial fitness for Sam, in turn, affected his level of fitness in other areas, such as his relationship with his wife, Amy. Communication problems further intensified his inner sense of frustration and uncertainty about the future, which only magnified his inability to take control of his weight.

To begin taking control of his life and his future, Sam needed to set some very specific goals to improve communication with Amy, particularly in the area of finances. Sam and I immediately began setting several SMART goals to boost his financial fitness, followed by a few SMART goals to open up communication channels around those financial frustrations. Openly communicating with Amy led to even smarter goals and, more importantly, a stronger relationship.

I could also see how money and communication problems had affected his diet and exercise patterns. His drinking habit had been growing worse. He had begun to eat mindlessly and withdraw a bit, searching for privacy or comfort he could not find elsewhere. He did find solace on his patio, and we learned through some initial conversations that Sam needed a place to call his own, as most of us do. This place for Sam was his back patio, so I encouraged him early on to create an environment there where he could "get away" to find peace through all of the new changes and challenges about to take place in his life.

Because Sam didn't have a good handle on his negative emotions, he had become discouraged about continuing to pursue his dreams, was having trouble cultivating and maintaining a quality relationship with his mother, and had put off finding a church where he could plug in and grow. All of these issues weighed heavily on him, and it showed. Helping him identify some of the problems and clarifying what he could do to resolve them was an empowering exercise. His mind-set shifted and he had a more hopeful attitude about what he would be able to accomplish, both short- and long-term. He was motivated to start with the little steps he could take now toward the bigger changes he truly desired. I helped him see that *every* positive step he made would contribute to his weight loss success.

Throughout the remaining chapters, we will be following Sam's story. I want you to see how working through these eight steps strengthens Sam's motivation. I also want to share the struggles he encounters and the hurdles he overcomes in the process of getting his body, and his life, into shape.

Below is a goal flowchart I asked him to work through at our first meeting. Sam's ultimate goal, which he wrote in the large circle, was to lose eighty pounds. The eight fitness areas are offshoots underneath, like a supporting root system. We talked about each of the eight areas and which needed the most work. We also discovered areas that he thought didn't need much work but actually did. We established several goals for every fitness area and then chose one from each that he would work on for the next thirty days.

Following the circles down, you will see they lead to his physical fitness goal. By addressing his eight life fitness goals, he will be able to address his physical fitness goal. As he achieves all of these goals and adds new ones, he will make measurable progress toward his ultimate goal of losing eighty pounds.

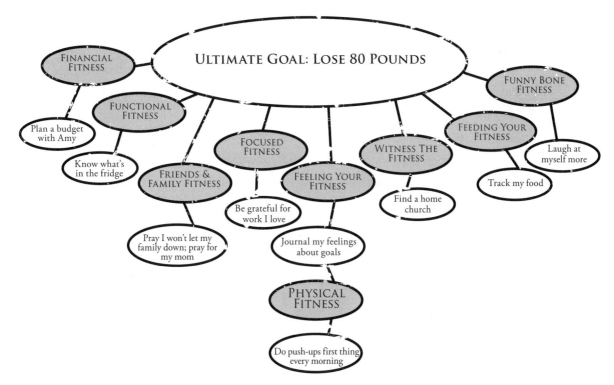

This flowchart shows how the eight *life* fitness area goals feed into the primary *physical* fitness goal.

Here are the eight life fitness goals Sam decided to work on the first month:

1 "Plan a budget with Amy." (Financial)

2 "Know everything in the fridge when asked." (Functional: Organizational)

3 "Pray I won't let my family down, and pray for my mom." (Friends and Family: Relationships)

4   "Be grateful every day for doing work I love." (Focused: Vocation)

5   "Journal my feelings regarding all of my goals." (Feeling: Emotions)

6   "Find a home church." (Witness the Fitness: Spirituality, Gratitude)

7   "Track my food." (Feeding Your Fitness: Nutrition)

8   "Laugh at myself more." (Funny Bone Fitness: Humility, Honesty, and Humor)

For physical fitness, Sam made it a goal to do push-ups first thing every morning. He'll begin with two regular push-ups and fifteen modified push-ups each morning. He will then add one more regular push-up every couple of days until he can do a total of fifteen regular push-ups. These goals are specific enough that action can be taken toward accomplishing each one every single day. They are measurable, attainable, and realistic because they identify a doable task that can be completed within a definable time frame.

You can begin setting these kinds of SMART goals for yourself by using the tools in the Appendix. This month, commit to working toward eight life fitness goals and one physical fitness goal. For physical fitness, you could begin with push-ups, or push-ups *and* a weekly exercise class (hopefully you're already doing your daily push-ups!).

> What you get by achieving your goals is not as important as what you become by achieving your goals.
>
> Zig Ziglar

WHERE THE RUBBER MEETS THE ROAD

Many people associate "getting motivated" with "getting in shape," and maybe that's what prompted you to pick up this book. That's a wonderful thing, and I want to help you get into the best shape possible! But I also want you to see that "being fit" is more than exercising and eating right. Sometimes the root of our "fitness problem" has more to do with our emotional or financial wellness than anything else. For me, getting my financial life in order has been a critical ingredient to my overall health and wellness. I recently read this statement by health activist Dr. Joseph Mercola: "It is impossible to separate your financial state from your health." Establishing financial fitness is our first area of focus on our goal flowchart, and it is probably the one area I have struggled with more than any other.

To help you become more financially fit and start setting some SMART goals in this area, I've enlisted the help of a client of mine, Kris, who is a financial advisor. I asked her three key questions about financial strength, and below are the eight motivating tips she gave me.

GUEST EXPERT MOTIV8N' MOMENT
FINANCIAL FITNESS

★ How do you define financial fitness?

1 If you are financially fit, you don't live paycheck to paycheck and you do live by a budget. This equals peace and not frenzied chaos. Planning ahead of time how you will save and spend money leads to a sense of control and well-being. You are financially fit when you are not overwhelmed by or emotionally strapped to money.

★ What are the most important things to do every day to grow financially stronger?

2 A precursor to any action steps would be to track your spending for forty-five days. Get a true concept of where your money is going so you can develop real financial goals. In other words, create a budget.

3 Treat money like food. Again, track it. Those who are aware of what they consume, be it food or money, tend to consume or spend less. Be as mindful of the money you are spending as you are of the calories you are eating.

4   In addition to writing down what you spend, be sure to keep your spending in line with your prepared budget, just as you would buy and prepare food in line with your healthy eating program.

5   Prepare for unplanned generosity. Open hands that readily give are therefore open to receive. Every day, look for ways to give. Random acts of kindness go a long way.

★ Give some examples of SMART financial goal prompts.

6   Get out of debt! Take all of your debts and list them from smallest to biggest. Start with the smallest amount and pay it off as soon as possible. This gives you a sense of success and a more positive outlook to help you tackle your larger debts.

7   Know what it will take for you to live for two to three months. Saving this amount of money in a reserve fund should be one of your primary goals.

8   Plan for your retirement as young as possible.

> The world makes way for the man who knows where he is going.
>
> Ralph Waldo Emerson

YOUR 8 SMART GOALS, PLUS ONE

Okay, now it's your turn. Write down at least one SMART financial goal. Make sure it is specific, measurable, attainable, realistic, and time-bound. Once you've done this, write down at least one goal for each of the other seven fitness areas, as well as a due date. These will evolve as we work through the next chapters. Also add one exercise goal (such as push-ups!). You will continue to use your goal chart and other tools as we explore each area in more detail.

1   Financial Fitness Goal

2   Functional Fitness (Organization) Goal

_____

3   Friends and Family Fitness (Relationships) Goal

_____

4   Focused Fitness (Vocation) Goal

_____

5   Feeling Fitness (Emotions) Goal

_____

6   Witness the Fitness (Spirituality, Gratitude) Goal

_____

7   Feeding Your Fitness (Nutrition) Goal

_____

8   Funny Bone Fitness (Humility, Honesty, Humor) Goal

_____

+1   Exercise Goal

_____

> You control your future, your destiny. What you think about comes about. By recording your dreams and goals on paper, you set in motion the process of becoming the person you most want to be.
>
> Mark Victor Hansen

CONSISTENCY CHALLENGE

Sometimes changing the entire direction of your life is as easy as making one small change. Go ahead and find that small thing you don't do because for some reason you think you can't or maybe because you're too lazy or just not in the habit of doing it. Pick one small thing you will change—one small adjustment you can make—and be consistent with that *one* thing. This one new change will be a catalyst for the fifty other things you're hoping to accomplish. It all starts with one small step.

Pick one new thing this week you have been afraid of doing. Write it down, do it, draw strength from it, and then write to me about it (staci@motiv8nu.com).

_____

_____

_____

(Meanwhile, don't forget to do your push-ups!)

> Do it now. You become successful the moment you start moving toward a worthwhile goal.
>
> Author Unknown

So here I give you a special little secret.
Please, please, be thoughtful of how carefully you keep it.

You will find over some time,
positive thoughts and feelings and especially acts
will fill your life with all you may lack.

This year is a new beginning for you.
This new day the things you'll do
will show you the gifts you have inside,
the ones you have but continue to hide,
the gifts you find courage in to get you through the pain,
and the ones that make
sunshine out of nothing but rain.

Your new creed: "Believe in yourself" holds true and steadfast.
Bring with you the positive, and make changes last.
Set goals that are real and goals that are SMART,
and live and love with every ounce of your heart.

—Staci

No food tastes as good as
being healthy and fit feels.

CHAPTER 6
THINK ABOUT WHAT YOU WANT

> When you determine what you want, you have made the most important decision in your life. You have to know what you want to attain it.
>
> Douglas Lurtan

Next to setting SMART goals, the most powerful action step you can take to develop motivational STRENGTH is to intentionally *think about what you want*. In other words, focus your mind on what you truly want—and *not* on what you *don't* want.

Setting SMART goals is *the* primary power tool you can use to keep your thoughts pointed in the right direction. Without goals to dominate your focus, your thoughts will land on any old thing. Like Silly String, they'll spew all over the place. For your thoughts to work in your favor, they need to be governed by the goals you want to achieve, not by the gullies you want to avoid.

Whatever your mind dwells upon is what your thoughts and, subsequently, you will move toward. Your thoughts are like magnets. As Napoleon Hill once said, "Whatever the mind can conceive and believe, it can achieve." But the opposite is also true: Whatever the mind can ponder will cause it to wander until it has taken your life off yonder. (Yes, I made that up!)

Make your thoughts productive, not counterproductive. Don't be a victim of "stinkin' thinkin'." If your thoughts stink, so will your life. Sometimes the only way to keep from focusing on the negative things that would pull you off course is to focus on the daily, weekly, and monthly goals you've set for yourself. Keep those goals in front of you at *all* times.

Every time your mind wants to consider failure or fear, plaster it back on an immediate goal, such as eating clean. Rather than thinking about what you can't eat, think about what you can. (Check the Appendix for my top eight clean food picks.) What is the next clean thing you will eat? Think about it; plan it; look forward to it. Think about how wonderful you will feel at the end of the day because you stuck to your plan, how fantastic you will look at the end of the month because you followed through, how great succeeding will actually *be*. Put yourself there in your mind. And most importantly, *expect* to succeed.

World-renowned productivity consultant Denis Waitley states, "Our limitations and success will be based, most often, on our own expectations for ourselves. What the mind dwells upon, the body acts upon." If you allow your mind to dwell on failure—worrying about going broke or never getting married or not staying married—then chances are good you will experience failure. If you think success—being happy, having your hard work pay off, having fulfilling relationships—those are the things you will experience.

"Whatever you focus on manifests as reality in your life," writes Bill Harris, director of the Centerpointe Research Institute. "You are always focusing on something, whether you are aware of it or not. . . . The results you get are always the result of your focus." Harris explains that when your mind is focused on something, as powerful as that focus is, it cannot tell the difference between something you want and something you don't want. It's just this powerful machine, like an engine or a generator using energy to pull you toward whatever you think about, good *or* bad. "Your job," he writes, "is to learn how to direct this power by consciously directing your focus to the outcomes you want." He continues:

> The mind . . . doesn't ask whether you're focusing on [something]
> because you want it or because you do not want it. It ALWAYS assumes
> you want what you focus on and then it goes and makes it happen.

The more frequent and the more intense the focus, the faster and more completely you will create what you have focused on, which is why intense negative experiences create intense focus on what you do not want, and tend to make you re-create what you don't want, over and over.[15]

But there's more to all of this than simply training your mind to focus on what you want. Everybody talks about the law of attraction. There are so many books out there that resonate with this idea. The belief in the power of the mind over the material world is indeed part of the puzzle, but you can't throw out the value of hard work and determined effort. You can't sit in your living room and only think about your future taking shape. You have to proactively shape your future. Thinking is the *catalyst* for taking action, not a *substitute* for it.

Take responsibility for what you want by taking control of your thoughts, and then get out there and make it happen. Connect the sensation of "being" that you've imagined with the "doing" you are capable of. Involve yourself in learning the new skill or cultivating the relationship or exploring the options that will help you achieve your goals.

Remember the SMART goals I prompted you to list in chapter five? You should be focusing on achieving these goals within thirty days. If after a few months you haven't fulfilled your first five goals, it's time to reevaluate. We set ourselves up for success by breaking our big goals into chunks we can achieve in the immediate, foreseeable future. If we can't actually see and feel the achievement of our goals, we won't be able to focus on them for long, and if a goal can't hold our attention long enough for us to see it through, how can it be realistic? Breaking your goals down into bite-sized pieces will help you keep your thoughts disciplined, and disciplining your thoughts is the only way to discipline your body.

To reinforce these disciplines, I recommend daily to-do lists. I don't just write one thing down I need to have done by the end of the year. I write a list of what I need to do every single day to keep my thoughts focused on what I really want. You should too!

---

15. This and the preceding two quotations are from Bill Harris, "The Incredible Power of Focus," *Centerpointe Research Institute*, http://www.centerpointe.com/articles/poweroffocus.php (accessed April 10, 2009).

Think of that song by the Spice Girls with the line "Tell me what you want, what you really, really, want!" What *do* you want . . . really, really want? How are those desires fueling your goals? What are you doing today to focus your thoughts and advance your life in the direction of your dreams? Are you putting feet to those thoughts by acting on them?

> If one advances confidently in the direction of his dreams, and endeavors to live the life which he has imagined, he will meet with a success unexpected in common hours.
>
> Henry David Thoreau

LAYING TRACK

Your thoughts essentially lay the track that determines where your life train goes. Your train won't go far without track to carry it, but you don't want your train heading down just any stretch of track either. You've always got to keep a clear destination in mind. Here is where your choices and your destiny intersect, so be sure to line up your decisions with your desires.

Sales and motivational speaker Zig Ziglar tells a great story about how our desires impact our destiny. It goes something like this:

> On a stretch of railroad track some men were working hard under the sun. A beautiful private train came by, and a man shouted from inside the train in excitement, "Hey, Old Jim! Is that you?"
>
> Old Jim, who was hard at work, looked up and replied, "Hi, Joe! That's me, all right!"
>
> "Jim, why don't you come in here for a cup of coffee?"
>
> Jim hurried in with joy, as the sun was hot and he wanted to get into the air-conditioned cabin of this beautiful train. After about an hour or so,

Jim came out with Joe and they hugged as old friends would and parted ways. When the train left, the people around asked Jim, "Hey, Old Jim, isn't that Joe Murphy, the president of our railway?"

"Sure he is. We have been friends for twenty years now. In fact, we've known each other since the first day we started together working on the railroad."

"What? How is it, then, that he is now the president of the railway, while you are still working here?"

"The answer is very simple. On the first day we came to work, I came to work for $3.50 per hour, but Joe Murphy came to work for the railway."

Two men began their careers in the same place at the same time but ended up in very different places years later. How did this happen? It all started with their internal motivation, their core desires. One was motivated to one day be the president, and the other was motivated to earn an hourly wage. The first man's decision caused him to possess a different attitude and therefore take different actions than the man who decided he was only there to collect a paycheck.

What is your motivation? Are you motivated by a salary or by the approval of others, or are you passionate about the dream of running the railroad? Are you working for someone or some*thing* else, or are you working to maximize your own greatest potential? Is your desire dictated by an internal value or an external reward?

> To accomplish great things, we must not only act, but also dream; not only plan, but also believe.
>
> Anatole France

WAKE UP TO WHAT YOU WANT

Focusing on what we want doesn't always come easily. Going through bankruptcy was a wake-up call for me on a number of levels. Not only did I learn I needed to set smarter goals, but I was also forced to reevaluate what I really wanted. The first thing I did was move into an apartment closer to work. I cut my commute time from almost two hours a day to about fifteen minutes.

Soon afterward, I received an offer to work at Bally. One of my goals was to make more money, so I taught some group fitness classes to earn a little more. At this time, I met a man named Dr. Jack Barnathan, whose mentorship has radically changed my life. His personal training certification course was exceptional, and I ended up bringing half a dozen of my colleagues to his big conference in New York. Since then, he has brought me in to do motivational STRENGTH seminars for his wellness coaches and mentored me in the arenas of personal coaching and public speaking. It is largely because of his influence that I'm doing what I do today.

But now I'm getting ahead of myself.

Back at Blue Cross Blue Shield, where I was still working while I worked part-time at Bally, I was feeling increasingly uncomfortable with one of my colleagues. I was younger than this colleague and we were on the same level administratively, but I was full of fire and energy and ideas and was probably exhausting to someone who wasn't on the same wavelength. The awkwardness gave me the opportunity to reevaluate where I wanted to work.

I have always been very tied in emotionally to my physical surroundings. I almost become physically ill if I feel I'm not where I'm supposed to be, and that's how I was beginning to feel at that job. When I began to ask myself what I wanted, I started feeling as if there was something more. Funny how that works. I had a feeling down in my gut that there was another thing I should be doing. I'm not sure if the feeling causes big changes to take place, or if the big changes cause the feeling, but I *was* sure I needed to pursue something new.

What I wanted was something more interactive, an aspect of work I enjoyed at Bally. I put a lot of thought into leaving Blue Cross and working for Bally full-time.

The turning point came when I attended a conference hosted by Dr. Jack. When I asked what he thought I should do, he told me to follow my dream. And that's ultimately what I've been doing ever since.

The health educator position at Blue Cross was simply my stepping stone to becoming a full-time fitness trainer and soon fitness director, and then an opportunity opened up to run a large club in the city. Jack believed in me, and his belief helped me believe in myself.

As soon as I heard about an opening for the director position at the Century Club, I applied. I thought about what I really wanted and determined in my heart that this was it. When I got the job, I threw all of my energies into turning around their personal training business and soon tripled their revenues. I went from having eight instructors working for me to overseeing a growing staff of forty personal trainers!

But now here I was again commuting as a single mom. I was still living in Lombard, Illinois, when I took the job in Chicago. It wasn't long before I packed up all of our belongings in my little car and moved closer to work.

> No one can get anywhere unless he knows where he wants to go and what he wants to be or do.
>
> Norman Vincent Peale

TRAIN YOUR FOCUS

As you can see from my story and as you've probably noticed on your own journey, if you want to achieve your goals, you've got to train your focus. Now that you've prioritized what's important to you and set SMART goals to help you live them out, don't let your thought life sabotage your efforts. Put as much energy into continually focusing your thoughts on what you want, and taking them off of what you don't want, as you did on setting goals.

If you let it, your mind will run your body and your life amuck. Instead, think about things that will run your body and life toward your goals. Think about the times things went well. Meditate on the *positive* conversations you've had with those you love. Focus on how it felt when you were successful. Remember how life looked and how you felt during those times. Recall your energy level when you felt connected to those around you or felt aligned with your highest purpose. Who was with you and what were you doing? Be specific. Now take those memories and construct a picture of how a perfect moment in time would look and feel. Expand this picture and write a detailed description of your ideal day. Allow the ideal to dominate your thoughts.

_____

_____

_____

_____

_____

Your thoughts, emotions, and attitudes are hugely powerful. According to the law of correspondence, everything happening to you on the outside is due to something happening to you inside. When you realize your outer world is radically influenced by your inner world, you will be free to stop blaming others and making excuses. It sounds simplistic, but really, until you get a handle on how you think, you will continually be bound by thoughts of your own shortcomings or others'. As long as negative thoughts dominate your actions, you will never move in a positive direction.

Not long ago, while I was flipping through *Tennis* magazine, my focus landed on this heading: "Tame Your Inner Voice: Stop the Self-loathing and Learn to Let Your Mind Work for You." Below, in big, bold letters, was a quotation from the article: "Some players possess a voice that amounts to nothing short of an internal terrorist." This resonated with me. I knew many clients I trained and coached battled inner terrorists.

This article explains how to retrain your inner voice to work for you instead of against you by increasing your ratio of positive thoughts to negative thoughts. "Researchers studying athletes have discovered that a negative voice is more powerful than a positive one," writes Jim Loehr. "What this means is that for every negative message you send, several positive messages will be required to undo the damage. . . . It's much better to enlist your voice as a silent partner rather than an enemy."[16]

When you are able to harness the power of your thoughts, you will be able to accomplish extraordinary things. Tony Davies, an expert in the areas of leadership and personal development, writes, "Change the quality of your thoughts and you will change the quality of your life!" He explains, "By focusing exclusively on what it is that we truly desire, and by eliminating all thoughts of what we don't want, we can begin to shape, mold, and build our lives to our own specifications. . . . Davies outlines three things you can do now to build the life you desire: determine how your thoughts and attitudes are reflected in your current reality, take full responsibility for what's happening in your life, and make the necessary changes to achieve the external world you desire.[17]

Write down what you want; read what you've written, preferably out loud; and see yourself already having what you want. The more emotion you can bring to it, the better. Then, take whatever action is available to begin moving toward your desires. Some good times to do this reading and visualizing are when you first wake up and right before you go to bed. What do you want?

_____

_____

_____

Continue to ask yourself, "How can I do this?" or "How can I be that?" and put thought into answering those questions. By persistently asking these kinds of questions,

---

16. This and the preceding quotation are from Jim Loehr, "Tame Your Inner Voice," *Tennis Magazine*, August 2009, http://ybyl.com/wordpress/?p=412 (accessed September 3, 2009).

17. This and the preceding two quotations are from Tony Davies, "Universal Law Series: Law of Correspondence," *Ezine @rticles*, http://ezinearticles.com/?Universal-Law-Series---Law-of-Correspondence&id=111639 (accessed March 5, 2009).

you get your mind to focus on what you want to have, to do, or to be. Then your mind takes over and answers the questions, solves the problems, and creates what your heart truly desires.

It's really a matter of aligning your head with your heart. You just have to provide the focus, take whatever action presents itself, and be persistent. Your mind will find a solution to accomplishing any compelling desire your heart confronts it with. Sometimes it is only a matter of articulating that desire so the head can accurately process it and get to work creating the outcome.

> To be successful at cooking you have to have incredible hunger, no doubt about it, not just for food. . . . There's a hunger to want to become something, to contribute, to do something that's good in the world.
>
> Norman Van Aken

MOTIV8N' SAM

With my client Sam, however, it wasn't only a matter of helping him think about what he wanted and what he didn't want. Before we could get to that point, it was more of a process of getting him to slow down enough just to think.

I believe many of us have this same problem. We have not been taught to think, or to use our thoughts to create the change we want. We get busier, do more, and work harder, but we never stop to think about what we're doing and why.

I have found journaling to be a great tool in stimulating the thinking process. I encouraged Sam to make a regular practice of writing in a journal. He was resistant at first, and it took quite a while for him to get comfortable with the idea of journaling his emotions and thoughts. I bought him a small journal he could take with him anywhere and personalized it with my favorite quote: "Your destiny is not by chance—it is by choice." I hoped creating a special "gift journal" would somehow finagle him into writing down what was on his mind. It still took some time, but once he realized how important it was to me, he started to see the benefits of it for himself.

If you don't first stop and let yourself think, you cannot begin to formulate and produce change. Only after you have allowed the thinking process to begin in earnest will you understand what you truly want and be able to effectively differentiate it from what you don't want. Once you have identified the thoughts taking you toward what you want (and not toward what you don't want), you can begin filtering the productive thoughts from the counterproductive ones. You can refocus your thought patterns. After Sam and I identified what he truly desired—ranging from financial security to deeper spiritual and relational connection, not to mention his eighty-pound weight loss goal—we focused with laserlike intensity *only* on those things he wanted.

> People deal too much with the negative, with what is wrong. . . . Why not try and see positive things, to just touch those things, and make them bloom?
>
> Thich Nhat Hanh

ORDER YOUR LIFE BY ORDERING YOUR THOUGHTS . . . AND YOUR CLOSET

One of my very best friends, Stacy Kvernmo, is an organizational genius. She is my ying, and I am her yang. We compete together, work out together, and go to church together. We have taught each other so much about life, love, and living. Organizational fitness is one area in which she is a true champion.

Organizational fitness is what I call functional fitness. If you're not organized, your life will be chaos and anything but functionally fit. With any kind of fitness comes a certain order. A fit mind, as we have just discussed, is focused, and focus comes from ordering your thoughts. Nutritional fitness requires eating intentionally and with order. You can order your nutrition as you do your thoughts or your strength training. A fit and healthy home would also be a well-ordered one.

You can learn to get the most joy and energy out of your living environment, just as you do your meals, your exercise, or your mind, through organization. Functional fitness is about organizing your physical environment. "As with all things in life, organization is essential to high performance and time management," says my BFF Stacy. "Saving time for the important things in life is a direct result of an organized closet. You can free up so much energy in the long run just by investing a small amount of energy up front."

I've taken Stacy's advice and organized my entire walk-in closet, and boy does it feel (not to mention *look*) good! It's amazing what big benefits come from organizing one little space.

And that's only the beginning. If you can tackle your closet, you can tackle anything. I know you'll benefit from what Stacy has to share about getting your closet organized—in other words, functionally fit. We can all learn from her answers to my key questions about becoming more functionally fit.

GUEST EXPERT MOTIV8N' MOMENT
FUNCTIONAL FITNESS (ORGANIZATION)

★ How do you define functional fitness?

1 You are functionally fit when your working environment—your home, your closet, etc.—feed your motivation and don't deplete it. Do your spaces make you feel stronger and more empowered, or do they make you feel weaker and out of control?

★ What are the most important things to do every day to get stronger in the area of home organization?

2 Put your clothes back in their place right away. Do not leave them on the bedroom floor or in the laundry room for days.

3 Color order your clothes by season or style. This makes it easy to quickly find what you are looking for.

4 Use organizational furniture/bins for additional spaces. If you do not have room, put your off-season clothes in a plastic bin or large vacuum-seal bags to put away in storage until the seasons change.

5 After drying your clothes, fold or hang them up right away to avoid extra wrinkling.

★ Give some examples of SMART closet organizational goal prompts.

6 No clothes on the floor, ever.

7 Hang clothes right away after wearing or washing them.

8 Throw away, give away, or store unnecessary items currently in your closet to clear space every several months.

> Your outer world—your environment, the noise level, the relative calm or chaos in your life—is usually a reflection of your inner world, the degree of peace and equanimity you experience in your mind.
>
> Richard Carlson

VISUALIZE YOUR EXERCISE

Another time to practice ordering your thoughts and focusing on what you want is when you are working out. Do you haphazardly go through the motions, or do you engage the full power of your mind (and each individual muscle) as you complete every rep of an exercise?

Try this the next time you work out: Think about what you want your muscles to do. What do you want your exercises to accomplish? For example, if you are doing a back exercise, close your eyes and think about your back muscles. If you don't really know what they actually look like, look it up. Understanding the muscles you are trying to strengthen and being able to mentally dial in to them will accelerate your progress.

Think about the last time you did a back exercise. A lat pull-down, for example. Were you just allowing your arms to take you through the movement, possibly using a lot more of your body to compensate for your lack of back strength, or were you fully engaging your core? Your core is your center of strength, your center of power, and it is where all of your movements begin.

No matter what your next exercise is, visualize it. I mean really see it, use it, and think about the muscle at work. Think about changing it, strengthening it, and making it beautiful. Also, draw your navel into your spine, pull your shoulder blades down into your back pockets, lengthen your neck, raise your chin, and align your posture. And then let the magic happen.

> Imagination is the beginning of creation. You imagine what you desire, you will what you imagine, and at last you create what you will.
>
> George Bernard Shaw

8 Quick Training Tips

1   Exhale on exertion.

2   Keep your shoulders in your back pockets.

3   During lower body exercises, drive your energy through your heels as you push upward, and keep your knees behind your toes. Feel those glutes and hamstrings firing.

4   Draw your navel into your spine to help engage your core.

5   When on your back, press your spine to the mat while slightly rocking your pelvis up, making a little cup.

6   Do not fix your gaze on the ceiling during core moves. Instead, let your eyes follow the movement of your body or drop your chin slightly toward your chest and close your eyes.

7   When doing a traditional push-up, before you say, "I can't," make sure your hands are placed just a little outside your shoulders. A common mistake is to have your arms in too close (like at the edges of your yoga mat), which limits proper movement and increases your risk of shoulder injury. Avoid a diamond stance. If you want to do triceps push-ups instead, glue your elbows to your sides and push through the heels of your hands.

8   When trying side plank movements, scissor your legs with the top leg in front, *not* behind.

You are never, ever alone in your pursuit of greatness.

CHAPTER 7
REV UP YOUR RELATIONSHIPS

The most important single ingredient in the formula of success is knowing how to get along with people.

Theodore Roosevelt

To develop motivational STRENGTH, you not only have to set SMART goals and think about what you want. You also have to take the next action step and *rev up your relationships*. Your relationships not only reveal a great deal about you, but they also mold you. You are who you are because of your relationships. From family to friends to partners to spouses, the people you gravitate toward and surround yourself with—the people you look up to and who look up to you—create a web that either supports or entangles you.

Your relationships are a reflection of you, mirroring not only your life values but also how you value your life. People who are always in conflict with others are usually struggling with conflicts within themselves. People who are angry, impatient, unforgiving, or uncomfortable with others are, more often than not, angry, impatient, unforgiving, or uncomfortable with themselves. Relationships are a part of that outer world that reflects your inner world.

American columnist Sydney J. Harris once wrote, "It's surprising how many persons go through life without ever recognizing that their feelings toward other people are largely determined by their feelings toward themselves, and if you're not comfortable within yourself, you can't be comfortable with others." This is why I feel so strongly about health and fitness and, more specifically, motivational STRENGTH. It's because they are so influential on how you perceive yourself and your potential and in turn influence how you perceive your relationships. Think how much more peace and joy there would be in the world if people could find peace and joy within themselves.

Mahatma Gandhi got it right when he said, "Be the change you wish to see in the world." It all begins with how you see yourself and how you *choose* to *be* in the world. Author Richard Bach wisely noted, "Every person, all the events of your life, are there because you have drawn them there. What you choose to do with them is up to you."

Of all the choices you must make about how to invest your time and energy, *with whom* is among the most important. The depth and quality of your relationships, and of your friends themselves, determine the depth and quality of your life. "The quality of your life *is* the quality of your relationships," says Anthony Robbins. When times are tough, it is the strength of your relationships that will see you through.

On the other hand, the hurts and sorrows of painful relationships will pull you under faster than anything else will. You might lose your job, but when you have people you can lean on and who will share the burden of challenging circumstances, you can get through the worst of times with your sanity intact. But losing a friend or business partner or being in conflict with your spouse can be more devastating than just about anything else.

The power of relationships can empower us as individuals, or it can weaken and weary us. In fact, sometimes the relationships that buoy us and make us stronger are the very same ones that can utterly destroy us. It's a paradox that what makes us invincible also makes us vulnerable. Those close to you have the power to direct the inner voice playing in your mind telling you you're either fabulous or a failure, so make sure you surround yourself with people who cause your mind to echo thoughts of greatness. Surround yourself with people who cause you to reach higher and do better, who raise the bar of your expectations for yourself and your community.

Staying connected to positive people is one of the most important things you can do to keep your thoughts, and your life, moving in the right direction. Tim Irwin, author of *Run With the Bulls Without Getting Trampled*, writes, "The key to sustaining change is accountability in a supportive environment." Who are you accountable to, and who is accountable to you? Those unspoken agreements about what we expect from those closest to us, and what they expect from us, are among the strongest transformational forces known to humanity. According to Irwin, they are "critical in forming and cementing changed behaviors so that they become habits."[18]

Having a friend accompany you on the uphill journey of change makes the climb less challenging. This is even true with friendships formed in supportive online communities. I know this is why so many of my online clients experience such great success. Through my Web site, motiv8nU.com, they find a network of support and accountability they wouldn't otherwise be open to in a face-to-face situation. In Web-based groups people find the safety of anonymity, yet also the comfort, accountability, and support of community.

Whether online or in person, healthy relationships are ones that will help you reach your goals. We all need this type of connection and community.

> We were born to unite with our fellow men, and to join in community with the human race.
>
> Cicero

THE POWER OF CONNECTIVITY

Friends and family are what make life meaningful and satisfying. Staying connected is one of the most healthful and energizing activities human beings can engage in. When we feel disconnected from loved ones, or even society at large, all sorts of negative feelings begin to emerge. We not only feel demotivated, but we can also become depressed or, worse, self-destructive.

Lack of social support and loneliness are among the leading causes of depression.

---

18. This and the preceding quotation are from Tim Irwin as quoted by Marshall Goldsmith, "The Power to Change," *Bloomberg Businessweek*, April 11, 2007, http://www.businessweek.com/careers/content/apr2007/ca20070411_924286.htm (accessed May 1, 2009).

According to psychologists Bob Murray and Alicia Fortinberry, founders of the Uplift Program, "Depression will be the second largest killer after heart disease by 2020—and studies show depression is a contributory factor to fatal coronary disease." They go on to say that good relationships are the cornerstone of mental *and* physical health. "Studies show . . . a supportive social network results in physical and emotional healing, happiness, and life satisfaction, and prevents isolation and loneliness, major factors in depressive illness."[19] Murray and Fortinberry explain that because human beings are genetically geared to live in socially interdependent settings, they are inherently relationship-forming creatures. Without a network of relationships, they wither and die much like a plant or tree that is separated from its root system. But as a broken branch can be grafted into a tree and begin to grow again, so can we find vitality when we are reconnected to a supportive community.

> Positive relationships can help reprogram the brain by stimulating new neural connections. Research suggests that a nurturing relationship environment can even undo the neural damage caused by childhood trauma by stimulating neurogenesis, or cell growth. That good relationships are the key to healing depression—as they are in preventing heart disease and even slowing the HIV virus—is not surprising.[20]

A study at the University of Chicago concluded, "Improvements in a sense of social connectedness may have clinical benefits comparable to, if not greater than, lifestyle modifications."[21] Caring relationships contribute not only to the prevention of illness but also to its cure.

On a larger scale, caring relationships have been attributed to the prevention of crime and heralded as the cure to risk behaviors among youth. In a report compiled by Dartmouth Medical School, the Institute for American Values, and the YMCA, it was discovered that the rising rates of emotional and behavioral problems among teens was the result of a pervasive lack of connectedness. The report, titled *Hardwired to Connect*, was the product of a team of thirty-three distinguished medical doctors,

---

19   Bob Murray and Alicia Fortinberry, "Depression Facts and Stats," *Uplift Program*, updated January 15, 2005, http://www.upliftprogram.com/depression_stats. html (accessed April 3, 2009).

20   Bob Murray and Alicia Fortinberry, "Depression: A Social Problem with a Relationship Solution," *The AHP Perspective Magazine*, June/July 2004, http://www. ahpweb.org/pub/perspective/june2004/june04cover.html (accessed April 3, 2009).

21   Melissa McNamara, "Loneliness Related to Blood Pressure?" *CBSNews.com*, March 28, 2006. http://www.cbsnews.com/stories/2006/03/29/health/webmd/ main1453783.shtml (accessed April 3, 2009).

research scientists, mental health professionals, and youth counselors who set out to discover why depression, suicide, and violent behavior had reached pandemic proportions in the U.S. They learned that at the center of this dilemma was a lack of connectedness, not only to other people but also to a higher purpose. "We mean two kinds of connectedness—close connections to other people and deep connections to moral and spiritual meaning." The researchers looked at the science behind the power of connection on both levels:

> . . . the human child is "hardwired to connect." We are hardwired for
> other people and for moral meaning and openness to the transcendent.
> Meeting these basic needs for connection is essential to health and to
> human flourishing.[22]

Our relationships affect every aspect of our lives. Think back to the eight areas of fitness: finances, organization, relationships, vocation, emotions, spiritual wellness, nutrition, and humor. Our relationships will determine our level of fitness in each one. In their book *Creating Optimism: A Proven, Seven-Step Program for Overcoming Depression*, Murray and Fortinberry offer the following explanation:

> . . . our ability to relate to other humans is our strongest survival
> mechanism. Without that ability we become prone to illness, depression,
> low self-esteem, and unfulfilling or possibly failed careers. Shared beliefs
> and rituals are vital to our spirituality. In short, relationships are central
> to everything that makes life worth living.[23]

No doubt the strength of our connection determines the strength of our health and well-being: spirit, mind, and body. The stronger and deeper our connections, the more resilient we will be, both as individuals and as a society. Interestingly, Franklin D. Roosevelt, president during both the Great Depression and World War II, wisely observed, "Today we are faced with the preeminent fact that, if civilization is to survive, we must cultivate the science of human relationships."

---

22. This and the preceding quotation are from "Hardwired to Connect: The Scientific Case for Authoritative Communities," *AmericanValues.org*, http://www.americanvalues.org/ExSumm-print.pdf (accessed April 3, 2009).

23. Murray and Fortinberry, "Press Release: Caring Relationships Crucial to Healing," *Uplift Program*, March 12, 2004. http://www.upliftprogram.com/press_release_040312.html (accessed April 3, 2009).

> The true sense of community lies in understanding our interconnectedness and acting from a sense of relatedness. . . . That is where we can start to reweave the sacred web of life so that it once again becomes whole.
>
> Suzanne Arms

BUILDING RESILIENCY

When people learn about some of the things I've gone through in my life, they often ask how I'm so resilient. I asked myself this question a lot, actually. I have always felt I could bounce back from anything and that I was tougher than my circumstances. *But why?* What did I have that made me particularly resilient? Is resiliency something we're born with, or is it a result of our environment?

As much as I wanted to learn how to motivate people to move forward, I wanted to learn how to help them bounce back from setbacks as well. I wanted to understand what had made me resilient so I could teach others to be also. As I mentioned, I had discovered that motivational STRENGTH comes from within a person; it's a matter of strengthening the *internal* connections of the heart, will, and emotions. What I now was learning was that *resiliency* is really a product of the number and degree of *external* connections a person has.

For a kid, these connections form a network of relationships beyond immediate family and close friends. They include teachers, coaches, supervisors, counselors, aunts, uncles, and grandparents, just to name a few. When I think back over my childhood, I remember many adults who spoke into my life over the years. For as many homes as I moved in and out of, schools I attended, and jobs I tried, I was connected in some meaningful way, even if briefly, to all of the people those places represented. These relationships are why I believe I was always able to bounce back.

The more assets kids have while growing up, the more resilient they will be throughout life. The Search Institute found evidence of this in a study that identified forty developmental assets that promote positive development in young people. External assets, which refer to the support and opportunities provided by family, friends, organizations, schools, and faith communities are what determine internal assets, which focus on the capacities, skills, and values needed to develop character and resiliency. According to Eugene Roehlkepartain and Dr. Peter Scale, authors of *Developmental Assets: A Framework for Enriching Service-Learning*, "The more assets young people experience, the *less* likely they are to engage in a variety of high-risk behaviors and the *more* likely they are to engage in thriving behaviors."[24]

With all of this in mind, imagine how difficult it would be to build motivational STRENGTH without a network of strong relationships. Without them, you wouldn't have the resiliency you need to stay motivated. Resiliency fuels motivational STRENGTH, and vice versa. The more motivated you are, the more resilient you'll be.

One essential key to staying motivated and bouncing back, then, is to maintain a network of healthy relationships. To keep those relationships going strong, you have to nourish them with good communication. Just as healthy eating habits boost your body's immune system, healthy communication habits boost a relationship's immune system. It's simple: Quality relationships are a result of quality communication.

> Man does not need to go to the moon or other solar systems. He does not require bigger and better bombs and missiles. His real need, his most terrible need, is for someone to listen to him, not as a "patient," but as a human soul.
>
> Taylor Caldwell

MOTIV8N' SAM

When I first met Sam, we talked a lot about his wife, Amy, and how supportive she

24. Eugene C. Roehlkepartain and Peter C. Scales, "Developmental Assets: A Framework for Enriching Service-Learning," *Learn and Serve Clearinghouse*, December 2007, http://www.servicelearning.org/instant_info/fact_sheets/cb_facts/developmental_assets/, (accessed April 2009).

is. When I met her, I could see that they have an amazing relationship—powerful and connected. So I wanted Sam to focus on recognizing and appreciating the great thing he already had and to continue nurturing it.

Early on, Sam and I decided to include Amy in every aspect of Sam's training. This really was an afterthought and not at all our initial intention. However, by the end of our first consultation, we decided to make Amy part of every training session. It has proven to be one of the best decisions we could have made. This, of course, meant total communication about every phase, goal, strategy, and "issue" Sam had to deal with in taking ownership and responsibility for himself and his family.

As we dug deeper into these issues, I discovered that Sam was very protective of Amy, not in a controlling way but from the standpoint of being her man and wanting the best for her. So we talked about how openly communicating can be one of the most protective things a person can do. As a result, we decided to include Amy even more in Sam's training. For example, with the financial decision-making process, Amy was part of the savings, investment, retirement, and insurance planning.

Thankfully we were not looking at a relationship with a lot of struggles, so the tweaking we did just strengthened an already solid structure. But as I have found, what you don't strengthen becomes weaker. Like any muscle, if you don't exercise it, it will atrophy. For Sam, then, our focus was not only recognizing a good thing but nurturing it.

> One of the greatest gifts you can give to anyone is the gift of attention.
>
> Jim Rohn

NOURISH RELATIONSHIPS THAT NOURISH YOU

I learned the hard way that it's important to nourish the right relationships, not the wrong ones. After I started working at the Century City Bally and moved to downtown

Chicago, I developed two totally different types of relationships: one good and the other not so good. A series of events transpired as a result of my new job and location.

About this time my ex-husband, Rolf, had gotten back in touch to become more involved in Corbin's life. He had begun paying child support, and I agreed to let Corbin go visit for the summer.

While Corbin was away those couple of months, I started going out at night with a new friend from the health club. She and her husband would host wild parties. I started to get heavily into that whole party scene and "letting loose." Looking back, I'm sure the only reason I did it was because I could. I was alone for the first time without my son, single, having been through some pretty rough years after leaving the Navy, and now feeling a little celebratory and loving my new life at Bally and in the city. So I partied.

My relationship with this "friend" was based entirely on the party scene. In fact, no one I normally spent time with even knew her. My socializing with her was completely separate from my time with my usual circle of friends. Leading up to this, I had been doing fitness tips on a local news show every Monday morning. I was kind of in the spotlight, and I think she thought I was cool. I was contributing to the newspaper and the Bally performance team. I had also been working with Dr. Jack Barnathan through N.Y. Strength, helping facilitate some conferences in Chicago and New York.

As the two months of Corbin's time with his dad began winding down, so did my interest in this new friend and her scene. I knew I couldn't live this kind of life when Corbin returned, so as quickly as I got into it, I got back out. I never looked that direction again.

Corbin's return was not the only factor redirecting my focus. I was also now dating my soon-to-be husband, Scott Boyer. We'd had our first accidental date on the Fourth of July. I had known him for a few years from Bally and remembered him watching our performance team routines at the Taste of Chicago. I had always thought he was cute, but my friend who was the head of the dance team thought she might be interested in him, so when we all went out, I only went along to support her. One night we went to a bar called the Bar Celona. I remember the bartender, who was a friend of mine, asking me if Scott was my boyfriend, and I told him, "No, he's not my boyfriend; he's just some guy I know from work." Well, later that evening we ended up walking and holding hands—linking pinkies, actually (everybody still teases us about it). Afterward, we went to Big City Tap in Chicago, and about midnight we had our first kiss. Thirty days later we were married.

We had flown to Vegas for a friend's wedding, but when I told my friends we were going, they just knew we would come back married. That was six years ago. We had a wonderful reception back home for all of our family and friends, in addition to the fourteen friends who were with us in Vegas as "Elvis" walked me down the aisle—the very same aisle Bon Jovi walked down when he got married. In our estimation, Elvis plus Bon Jovi had to mean wedded bliss!

Not long after Scott and I were married, I started training Lauren Cohn and Art Norman from two TV stations in Chicago, and the next thing you know I was flying to New York for the *Caroline Rhea Show*.

At this point, Scott was general manager of another Bally. I was the fitness director at Century, working all the time. Scott said to me one day, "You know, you don't have to work so much. Why don't you step down and enjoy being with Corbin for a while?"

I thought, *This is great! This is the man I have been looking for. All right, I can step back; I can do that.* I was thankful to have a man in my life to take care of things.

So I quit working at the club in the city, and Scott and I decided to move to the suburbs. So not only did we feel suburbia would be better for Corbin, but I also wanted to be closer to Lish, who was going through a divorce. She had been, and still is, one of my closest friends and was really going through a difficult time. So this is how we ended up in Naperville.

Eventually I started teaching group exercise classes at the local health club and was soon approached by the district manager with an offer to take over the fitness director position. Apparently some issues needed to be fixed, and he wanted to know if I was up for the challenge. I agreed to take the job, went in, and cleaned house. This was not an easy task, and it caused me some sleepless nights that I will not soon forget.

Scott was working a part-time bartending job and really felt there was another place for him in his future other than Bally, so after I started working full-time again, we decided it would be a good idea to explore other options. And of course, as luck would have it, that's when I got pregnant with Drew. (God gives us so many miracles in so many packages!)

Notice how important it is to support those people who nourish you. Being older now, I understand how very important these relationships are to my mental health. I understand the importance of having friends like Lish and other people who have been there for me—those people who know me better than anyone else.

You don't have to have a lot of friends in your life, but you can honor those few who rely on you to be there through thick and thin and the people you know will be there for you. Everyone needs people to confide in. You may not talk with them every day, but you need to have someone in your life with whom you can always pick up where you left off no matter how much space or time comes between you. I think it's essential to always know there is someone on the planet with whom you can be yourself, someone who sees you for who you really are and loves you that way. Someone with whom you don't have to pretend you are happy when you're not. Someone who, no matter what you're going through, will always be there to listen to you and never judge you. Those people make more difference in our lives than most of us ever imagine.

> The greatest happiness of life is the conviction that we are loved—loved for ourselves, or rather, loved in spite of ourselves.
>
> Victor Hugo

RAIN-RESISTANT RELATIONSHIPS

Some friends come in disguises. The person with whom I have probably been the angriest has turned out to be one of the most influential people in my life. It all started during a house hunt.

When Scott and I decided to move to the suburbs and started looking for a house, we found one that needed a lot of work, but we could get it for a good price and Scott was willing to put in the labor. My friend was acting as our real estate agent. We were trying to close on the house and couldn't figure out what was going wrong. All the while, my relationship with this real estate friend was rapidly deteriorating.

Our lease was up, so we took a leap of faith and agreed to move into this fixer-upper before closing and proceeded to blindly and ignorantly make improvements on the property over the course of the next two months. Taking money out of Scott's 401k, we invested twenty thousand dollars in the remodeling. After we had agreed to buy the house, put our money down, and secured a loan, the house was reappraised for more than we could afford. We had not actually signed a contract yet, only a lease agreement, so when we called the sellers to tell them we couldn't pay the new asking price, they threatened to sue us. Since we didn't have a contract, they couldn't follow through with it, but there was no way to recover the money we had put into the house either. At that point, we cut our losses and left. We were devastated. Not only had Scott put so much heart and labor into renovating the house, but we'd also lost all of that money. I felt completely misled and betrayed by my real estate agent friend and wasn't able to forgive her for a long time.

I learned a lot from this experience. First, I learned it's important to always educate yourself and not rely on someone else to do your thinking for you. There were some unusual extenuating circumstances I can't completely blame on my friend, and I believe now she did the best she could with what she understood at the time. I also learned to not judge anything from appearances. I'd judged the house and sellers completely wrong, and my friend had too. As it turned out, my friend had only wanted the best for us and has since seen us through some really rough spots. She also talked a lot with me about my life and invited me to church. Though I didn't go with her, I actually did end up going to church with another friend and am now really involved there. If it hadn't been for going through what we did with my real estate friend, I may never have been open to that.

The point is that you can go through some real highs and lows with folks, and that's what makes those relationships deeper and richer. I've seen it firsthand.

We eventually found a cute town house in Naperville near my friend Lish's place, and today we have a supportive circle of friends we are committed to sticking by no matter what life throws at us.

When I think about the people who are most important to me and have been there through everything—the good, the bad, and the ugly—I have to admit not every season of those relationships was easy or joyous, but the friendships endured. They were built on something more than a good time or a party or looking cool.

I can unreservedly say that if it weren't for those people in my life, I wouldn't be who I am. I think of my stepmother, who held our family together after my father died, of all the wonderful things I've learned from her about how to keep it together during times of adversity. I am so grateful for her presence in my life and what she has taught me about being resilient. I remember my grandmother, who was such a pillar of strength and beauty and who laid the foundations of honor and integrity in me that will ripple through generations. And there have been so many more who have built my resiliency.

Think of the people who have helped you bounce back during hard times, and then remember the mark you leave on the lives you touch. Never underestimate the power of love to heal any wounded heart (including your own).

> You can kiss your family and friends good-bye and put miles between you, but at the same time you carry them with you in your heart, your mind, your stomach, because you do not just live in a world but a world lives in you.
>
> Frederick Buechner

My real estate friend has actually been the one who has mentored me in the area of relationships. She and her husband have been an amazing source of insight and information about strengthening relationships with those we love—and even those we don't. They have done a great deal of coaching, counseling, and speaking in regard to improving communication and building healthy relationships. So I asked her how to become more relationally fit. Here's how she responded to my three key questions.

GUEST EXPERT MOTIV8N' MOMENT
FRIENDS AND FAMILY FITNESS (RELATIONSHIPS)

★ How do you define friends and family fitness?

1 Friends and family fitness requires purposefully prioritizing the significant relationships in our lives so we are giving our best self to those who matter most.

★ What are the most important things to do every day to strengthen relationships?

2 Ask yourself who and what are most important to you. Spend your time and talents and give your best to them. Be "in the moment." Put the true "first things" first. Life is too short to waste on things that won't matter a month from now.

3 Communicate. Don't let fear or apathy prevent you from admitting you were wrong or from saying, "I'm sorry," or "I love you." If you don't, you can make others afraid to talk to you. Be approachable. Conflict is inevitable.

4 Cultivate an "attitude of gratitude." Be thankful for the people in your life and focus on the many *good* things they bring to the relationship.

5 Always be honest. Share how you feel, what you need, and what you expect. Then set goals to accomplish those things. Those goals might be small or large, present or future, easy or challenging. Little victories are the seeds of great accomplishments.

★ Give some examples of SMART relationship fitness goal prompts.

6   If you're not green and growing, you're ripe and rotting. Invest in yourself. Expand your world. Do one thing a year that you would never normally do to grow as an individual. Nothing kills a relationship like becoming bitter from losing yourself.

7   Do one thing a year to make your marriage better and stronger. Go to a marriage conference or read a book with your spouse. Do something to grow in your relationship. Again, if you're not growing, you're rotting.

8   Regularly do a checkup on your relationships to reassess your priorities.

★ BONUS: What are your top 8 quick tips to keep relationships on the right track?

1   Put first things first. Purposefully invest your best self in the relationships that mean the most to you. Remember: You will not be here forever.

2   Remember that it's not always about you. Know when to give someone space. They may just figure it out themselves.

3   Pray often—for others and for yourself. Pray together. Never underestimate the strength of a praying family.

4   Always forgive. You're not perfect either, and two imperfect people will never have a perfect relationship. Bitterness is like swallowing poison and expecting someone else to die.

5   In any relationship, remember that you're both on the same team with the same goal. A team divided never wins.

6   Remember that love is a verb. Don't just tell people you love them. Show them, even when you don't feel like it. Love is more than a feeling; it's a choice.

7   Visit a garbage dump with your family. Everything you have ever owned or will ever own will eventually end up here. Marriages, families, and friendships have been destroyed over "stuff" that inevitably ends up in the garbage. *Love* the people in your life, and *use* the things you have. Not the other way around.

8   Have fun. Enjoy each other!

> When you look for the good in others, you discover the best in yourself.

Martin Walsh

RESILIENCY MEMORIALS

When I think of the times I wanted to give up, I think about the people who saw me through. When you've had rough times, who were the people who helped you become resilient? Think of the times you bounced back, and acknowledge that ability in yourself and those who had a part in instilling it in you. When you give yourself credit for bouncing back, it will give you courage to move forward and become even more resilient in the future.

I want you to create a resiliency memorial by writing down a specific situation you faced and how you got through it. Perhaps you were faced with bankruptcy and, whether you filed for it or you didn't, you are still here to talk about it. It may have been difficult, but you survived.

Hey, I know! I've been there. I have lost two houses, one through foreclosure and the other I mentioned in the last few pages, and to this day I still don't own my own home. Am I a success or a failure? Some would say I'm a failure because of the loss, but I've bounced back from both and have moved on stronger than ever. I say that those experiences have made me more resilient and are memorials for me to look back on and say, "If that didn't get me down, then I can handle this. If I can endure that, then I can endure anything." I know the people who were there through it all and my supportive friends will continue to build my resiliency.

If you have faced bankruptcy, foreclosure, divorce, or the loss of a job and survived, I want you to recognize it. Write it down. What did you do to overcome during moments of weakness? Now pat yourself on the back. I want you to be proud of yourself for doing that. You have resilience. And you can be sure the people around you are proud of you!

Write down a situation in which you demonstrated resiliency. Then write down a time when you weren't so resilient. What was the difference? Who were the people around you when you weren't resilient? What could they/you have done differently?

_____

_____

_____

_____

_____

What is one thing you can write down here, one quote or thought or song lyric, that will help you be resilient next time you are faced with adversity?

_____

_____

_____

_____

_____

Your destiny is not by chance—it is by choice. It is clearly your choice to either be resilient or not. It is not someone else's choice. It's yours. If you want to get up and shake it off, that's your choice. Every time.

> Go out into the world today and love the people you meet. Let your presence light new light in the hearts of people.
>
> Mother Teresa

LIST 8 PEOPLE WHO HAVE HELPED MAKE YOU GREAT.

_____

_____

_____

_____

LIST 8 PEOPLE YOU ARE HELPING BECOME GREAT.

_____

_____

_____

_____

It's not about gimmicks.

*It's about cultivating
the gifts you're blessed with.*

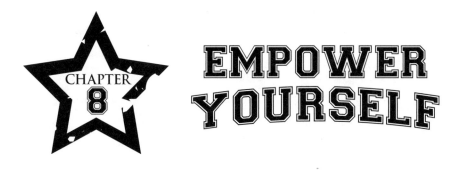

EMPOWER YOURSELF

CHAPTER 8

> Strong lives are motivated by dynamic purposes.
>
> Kenneth Hildebrand

You've seen that to develop motivational STRENGTH, you need to set SMART goals, think about what you want, and rev up your relationships. The next action step you need to take is to *empower yourself.*

Empowerment comes from our ability to connect with and act upon our innermost drives and desires. This connectivity fuels our motivation to change and grow and explore the limits of our greatest potential. We connect with what is best in ourselves through our connections with what is best in those around us.

As we've seen, our relationships help us identify and define what truly motivates us, affirm what is meaningful to us, strengthen what is good in us, and adjust those things that might not be so wonderful about us. One proverb says, "As iron sharpens iron, so a friend sharpens a friend."[25] Our inner convictions are sharpened, or strengthened, as a result of our outer connections. Our friends and family mold and shape our values and help us find relevance and meaning in our lives.

Beyond our interpersonal relationships, however, lies the deep connection we have to the rest of humanity. When we are motivated to pursue a goal on behalf of others, we are tapping into an exponentially more powerful motivational force. True empowerment comes not by serving oneself but by serving others, not by being motivated *because* of others as much as on *behalf* of others.

Author of *The Power of Positive Thinking*, Norman Vincent Peale, wrote: "When you

---

25. *Holy Bible: New Living Translation* (Wheaton, Ill.: Tyndale House, 1996, 2004), Proverbs 27:17.

become detached mentally from yourself and concentrate on helping other people with their difficulties, you will be able to cope with your own more effectively. Somehow, the act of self-giving is a personal power-releasing factor." Author Tim Irwin concurs: "The most notable changes seem to occur when someone connects with a deep inner commitment to a purpose such as making a difference in the lives of others." There is something empowering about knowing you are a positive force in the world and your presence on the planet makes a difference.

As you've learned, motivation is "something that energizes, directs, and sustains behavior." In this chapter, I want to explore motivation and show you how it works and how to increase and harness it so that you can be empowered to face every challenge. The force of motivation is unique to you, and it is your gift to the rest of the world. It will bring energy and joy to you and everyone around you when you learn to tap into it and really flow with the power it offers.

Author and teacher Shakti Gawain has said, "When I'm trusting and being myself as fully as possible, everything in my life reflects this by falling into place easily, often miraculously." Actress Barbara Cook advises, "If you're able to be yourself, then you have no competition. All you have to do is get closer and closer to that essence."

What is that essence? I call it empowerment. Some call it genius.

In *The War of Art: Break Through the Blocks and Win Your Inner Creative Battles*, Steven Pressfield explains the word *genius*:

> Genius is a Latin word; the Romans used it to denote an inner spirit,
> holy and inviolable, which watches over us, guiding us to our calling. A
> writer writes with his genius; an artist paints with hers; everyone who
> creates operates from this sacramental center. It is our soul's seat, the
> vessel that holds our being-in-potential, our star's beacon and Polaris.[26]

I thought this was really a beautiful description of the energizing force unique to each of us, the *essence* Barbara Cook spoke of, the inner power compelling us to act, the force that "energizes, directs, and sustains behavior."

This is motivational STRENGTH, and now we're going to delve into the

---

26. Steven Pressfield, *The War of Art: Break Through the Blocks and Win Your Inner Creative Battles* (New York: Grand Central Publishing, 2002), Preface.

mechanics—get into the nuts and bolts, so to speak—of how to develop deep and dynamic motivational STRENGTH. It all starts with our motivations. Remember: our ability to connect with and act upon our innermost drives and desires will determine how empowered we are to reach our dreams.

> When we are motivated by goals that have deep meaning, by dreams that need completion, by pure love that needs expressing, then we truly live life.
>
> Greg Anderson

WHAT MOTIVATES YOU?

Motivational STRENGTH is derived from two sources: your inner convictions and your outer connections. These two forces fuel each other while also providing two distinct types of motivational power: intrinsic and extrinsic.

Knowing what motivates you on different levels, and why, is a key component of successfully empowering yourself over the long run. When we have a firm grasp on *why* we want to do something from an intrinsic perspective, we will be empowered to work through the *how* on a more extrinsic level.

For example, if I want to have more energy to help people (which is what intrinsically motivates me), then I might use some kind of extrinsic motivator, such as improving my performance in the next triathlon, as the *how* to fulfill my *why*. Extrinsic motivators can be useful tools if intrinsic ones prompt them—in other words, if the primary motivation is an internal desire to pursue a goal because the pursuit itself brings pleasure. Psychologist and child development expert Carol Bainbridge defines this driving force as the kind of motivation that "comes from the pleasure one gets from the task itself or from the sense of satisfaction in completing or even working on a task. . . . Intrinsic motivation does not mean, however, that a person will not seek rewards. It just means that such external rewards are not enough to keep a person motivated."[27]

Therein lies the key. If you want to empower yourself, you will need to develop your intrinsic motivators. Relying on external rewards, or extrinsic motivators, will only get you so far for so long, because the benefit you are deriving is unrelated to the thing you are actually doing. Bainbridge notes, "These rewards provide satisfaction and pleasure that the task itself does not provide."[28] If you are not getting pleasure out of what you are actually doing, you will only be committed to doing it for so long. Why place those limitations on yourself? Why sabotage your best efforts when you could turbocharge them by understanding and tapping into what energizes you intrinsically?

This is where you might need to change your perspective or do a little paradigm shifting. Try to see the bigger picture. Step back and appreciate the trajectory of your life as a whole. Some call this life mapping. Or look deeper to pinpoint that tiny spark of something flickering like a pilot light inside your soul. What energizes you? When have you felt most alive and in the moment? Whether you call it life mapping or soul-searching, you need to understand what really makes you tick.

Some people don't begin this process until they're in their forties or fifties, maybe even till after they retire; others seem to tune in to their inner passions and run with them right out of school. They don't have any trouble locating their North Star and following it. But wherever you are in the process, the more intrinsically motivated you are, the more successful you will be, on many different levels.

Your success is as much a state of mind as your destiny is your choice. Awareness is among the most critical methods to achieve any goal, *especially* weight loss. Empowerment involves heart-and-soul muscle. In fact, anything related to health, fitness, or lifestyle is solely (or soully) a matter of motivation.

To fuel that motivation you need to align your desires with a larger purpose, something bigger than you and your immediate experience.

We can either watch life from the sidelines, or actively participate. . . . Either

---

27. Carol Bainbridge, "Intrinsic Motivation," *About.com*, http://giftedkids.about.com/od/glossary/g/intrinsic.htm (accessed May 1, 2009).
28. Carol Bainbridge, "Extrinsic Motivation," *About.com*, http://giftedkids.about.com/od/glossary/g/extrinsic.htm (accessed May 1, 2009).

> we let self-doubt and feelings of inadequacy prevent us from realizing our potential, or embrace the fact that when we turn our attention away from ourselves, our potential is limitless.
>
> Christopher Reeve

ACTUAL VERSUS ACTUALIZED

Many people are extrinsically motivated, or primarily driven by external rewards because it is how many of us *learned* to be motivated. Motivation, like any other behavior, is learned. We are taught from a young age to modify our behavior based on external consequences. We grew up learning that for every action there is a reaction. So it makes sense that many of us naturally fall back on extrinsic motivators. We perform for approval. Our entire self-identity might be wrapped in a performance-based approval system or feedback loop.

So how do we move away from the quagmire of relying on extrinsic motivators to catching the currents and updrafts of our intrinsic motivators? How can we learn to spread our wings and ride the waves of what inspires us rather than taking refuge in what, dare I say, manipulates us?

Living with purpose and becoming empowered to be all that we can be requires that we become increasingly intrinsically motivated. Abraham Maslow brought the concept of self-actualization, a term first coined by Kurt Goldstein, to the forefront with the publication of his 1943 paper called "A Theory of Human Motivation." Self-actualization is the "motivation to realize own maximum potential and possibilities. . . . In Maslow's hierarchy of needs, the need for self-actualization is the final need that manifests when lower level needs have been satisfied."[29] According to Maslow, "This tendency might be phrased as the desire to become more and more what one is, to become everything that one is capable of becoming."[30]

---

29. *Business Dictionary*, s.v. "self-actualization," http://www.businessdictionary.com/definition/self-actualization.html (accessed May 1, 2009).

As Maslow studied this ultimate intrinsic need of every human being to become what they were meant to be, he discovered there were progressive levels of extrinsic needs that had to first be met. This led him to develop a "Hierarchy of Needs," which describes each of the five levels of needs an individual must progress through sequentially. The first level represents our physiological needs, or basic survival needs, such as food and shelter. If these basic needs aren't met, we won't be able to progress to the second level (safety), the third level (love and belonging), the fourth level (esteem), and certainly not the fifth level (self-actualization). This is why when we see homelessness, famine, or widespread disease or war, the affected individuals rarely become everything they are capable of becoming. Often, personal motivation and drive are lacking because the fulfillment of basic needs is lacking.

However, as individuals progress through these levels of having their needs met, they are able to move away from being motivated by purely extrinsic rewards (such as doing whatever it takes to survive) toward becoming more motivated by intrinsic rewards (such as the feeling of empowerment from volunteering for a cause they believe in). Actress Gillian Anderson once said, "Be of service. Whether you make yourself available to a friend or coworker or you make time every month to do volunteer work, there is nothing that harvests more of a feeling of empowerment than being of service to someone in need." If you want to discover the energizing force of intrinsic motivation and understand true empowerment, find something you can do for someone else.

One of the reasons I believe I was able to become more intrinsically motivated and empowered earlier on was that many of my physiological and safety needs were met in the Navy. I felt liberated and empowered to help others above and beyond the call of duty. This was probably the beginning of my being able to tap into what motivated me intrinsically and what enabled me to move forward with this kind of self-identity.

When did you feel most empowered and motivated by something beyond yourself? Ask yourself, and think about that answer. More importantly, do you have an answer? If not, I want you to keep working toward experiencing that motivation and empowerment.

Let's see how by taking a closer look at each of the levels in Maslow's Hierarchy of Needs.

---

30. A. H. Maslow, "A Theory of Human Motivation," *Classics in the History of Psychology* (originally published in *Psychological Review*, 1943: 83), http://psychclassics.yorku.ca/Maslow/motivation.htm (accessed May 1, 2009).

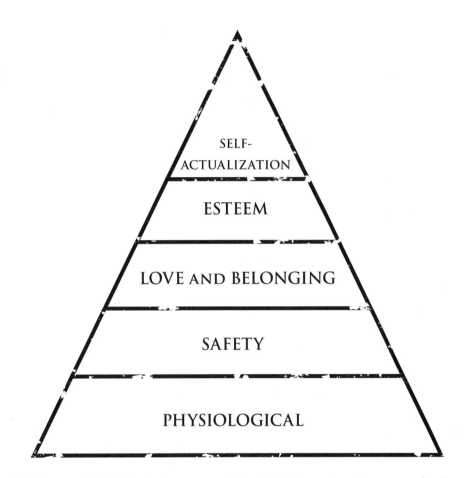

Maslow concluded that before we can be intrinsically motivated, we must first have our more basic human needs met. Once our first four levels of needs are satisfied, we're able to concentrate on functioning to our highest potential.

Although few ever self-actualize, Maslow admitted, our aspiring to do so is what makes life fulfilling. As a society we can help ourselves, our children, and each other satisfy our first four basic needs so everyone can share in this aspiration. Intrinsic motivation will not occur until an individual is fed, feels safe in his or her environment, and can give and receive love and respect. When these vital necessities are in place, the individual will have much more motivation and empowerment to embark on new life goals.

As you read this, you most likely have a place to live and enough food to eat. If so, then your first level of needs (physiological) is met. Maybe you feel relatively secure in your surroundings, your life is not at risk, and your home is not being threatened. However, if you are struggling with health issues or are in transition with your job or home situation, you might be stuck at the second level (safety). Or maybe you haven't been able to get past the third level (love and belonging) because you are insecure in your friendship situation, or relationship concerns are holding you back for some reason.

Now if you look back at those physiological, safety, and love and belonging needs, the motivation they bring is purely extrinsic. The intrinsic motivation comes with the next two levels: esteem and self-actualization.

At the fourth level, we begin thinking about what our emotions are doing as we move through this entire self-actualization process. We want to have good self-esteem and confidence. If we don't have a healthy self-esteem or positive perception of ourselves (the fourth level), we won't have the confidence we need to self-actualize (the fifth and final level).

As you develop courage and become empowered to pursue and achieve your goals, you develop faith in yourself. Without that faith, you can never become all you are capable of becoming, fulfill your greatest potential, or "self-actualize."

You will need to change how you see yourself if you are ever to see your best self.

> You have been criticizing yourself for years, and it hasn't worked. Try approving of yourself and see what happens.
>
> Louise L. Hay

LIVING FROM THE INSIDE OUT

I truly started feeling the most alive and empowered when I was in the Navy on the hospital ship in the Persian Gulf. I started to find my gifts as I began to get up in front of people and do some teaching. During my time on the USS *Emory S. Land*, I spoke on the flight deck, then taught and trained in the mess halls. Finally, I started working as a certified master trainer, doing instructor training in the hospital corps school.

I was able to say, "This is my spark; this is what I'm all about." When we are consciously able to say that, we begin to wake up to who we actually are—who, in essence, we were created to be. This realization is at the core of the self-actualization process. When we begin to operate from our "sacramental center," as Pressfield called it—our "soul's seat . . . that holds our being-in-potential,"[31] our true self begins to find expression and we are empowered to live to our fullest potential.

Whether you are skilled in music, art, writing, cooking, or something else, when you are able to let your genius emerge and reach for your best self with every fiber of your being, unreservedly and unselfconsciously, your true self will materialize, or actualize. And when this happens, you will be empowered to overcome every challenge and live to your highest potential.

What is your gift that you *have* to do to be fulfilled in life? Musicians must play music. Artists must create art. I must speak to people. When you know what you *have* to do, you will be intrinsically motivated to do it. When you discover that one thing— whether you are a speaker, a scientist, a painter, or a poet—you will have discovered why you are here and what your gift is to the world.

Whatever burns in you, no matter how small the ember is now, will continue to smolder throughout the rest of your life until you fan it into flame. In the poignant words of one of my favorite poets, Maya Angelou, "There is no greater agony than bearing an untold story inside you." I think we have all felt that agony at some time in our lives. What gift is burning inside of you? What do you need to become empowered to give to others through the venue of your gift?

Some of us need to go ahead and tell our story with confidence. It's almost as if the agony of not telling the story outweighs the agonizing fear of actually telling it. Believe it or not, I was always shy. So shy, in fact, that when I was in school, I would not enter a classroom after the bell rang because I didn't want to be noticed or called out. I also

---

31. Steven Pressfield, *The War of Art: Break Through the Blocks and Win Your Inner Creative Battles* (New York: Grand Central Publishing, 2002), Preface.

always, always sat in the back. It wasn't until I sort of discovered myself in the Navy through what interested me and what I was passionate about that I began sitting closer to the front in classroom settings.

That's what self-discovery will do for you. It will actually make you *less* self-conscious. You will be more concerned with doing what you're inspired to do than whether or not you succeed or fail. I once read the following statement by an unknown author:

> People who are too concerned with how well they are doing will be less successful and feel less competent than those who focus on the task itself. . . . Some psychologists call it a conflict between ego-orientation, or between extrinsic and intrinsic motivation . . . but in all cases, what counts is whether attention is turned away from the task at hand and focused on the self and its future rewards, or whether it is instead trained on the task itself. The latter attitude seems the more fruitful.

It's important to let go of *how* you are performing and instead focus on *why*. When you can do this, you will be more empowered and successful. In the Navy, I began focusing on the *why* rather than the *how*. Even after I left, I was driven to continue teaching and training and motivating, which is how I ended up doing group fitness and personal training at Bally. Somehow, working with groups of people and coaching one-on-one filled a need I didn't even know I had until years later. For me, nothing in this life brings more joy than helping people be the best they can be physically, mentally, and even professionally. I want to see people fulfill their greatest potential on every level. This is what excites me and empowers me to get up in the morning and do whatever needs to be done, to overcome obstacles and keep going no matter how inadequate I feel. What is it that empowers you?

Another remarkable poet and activist, Audre Lorde, once wrote, "When I dare to be powerful, to use my strength in the service of my vision, then it becomes less and less important whether I am afraid." And I like what the great motivational speaker Les Brown once said: "We all need some form of deeply rooted, powerful motivation—it empowers us to overcome obstacles so we can live our dreams."

> If I can stop one heart from breaking, I shall not live in vain; if I can ease one life the aching, or cool one pain, or help one fainting robin unto his nest again, I shall not live in vain.
>
> Emily Dickinson

MOTIV8N' SAM

When we look at the word *empower*, we often compare it to the word *enable*. Enabling someone to continue in a certain behavior, however, is *not* the same as empowering them to change. Too often when people are in need of making changes, what holds them back is an "enabler." This can be a person, a thing, or a situation. With Sam, for example, his previous job in the food industry had, in a sense, enabled him to make some unhealthy life choices.

It can become easy for any of us to "go with the flow" and allow people or circumstances to dominate our lives, but sooner or later we will wake up unhealthy, overweight, or frustrated. Maybe you have cramps for no good reason, an unorganized closet, no retirement plan, or no life insurance. It's amazing how one thing can lead to another. In Sam's case, we had to identify what the enablers were and neutralize them, while empowering him with the necessary tools to succeed.

We needed to empower Sam to change rather than enable him to remain as he was. We did this by shifting his primary motivators from extrinsic to intrinsic. The first step was simply teaching him what those motivators were. There is so much truth in the old saying "Give them a fish and they will eat for a day; teach them to fish and they will eat for a lifetime." I empowered Sam with what he needed to know to change his lifestyle overall. Not just for today but for every day.

I want to encourage you to identify what truly motivates you from deep inside so that you can begin to take the action step of empowering yourself to make positive changes in your life. Change is a lifelong process, and earning a degree from the school of hard knocks can take as long as earning a master's degree. It takes all of us years to become indoctrinated in how to *do things right*, instead of *doing the right things*, and it might take you time to reeducate yourself in what the *right things* are for you. By disengaging yourself from compromising enablers and embracing what truly empowers you, you *will* change.

> I wanted to change the world. But I have found that the only thing one can be sure of changing is oneself.
>
> Aldous Huxley

AN INTRINSIC NEED TO HELP OTHERS

So there I was teaching at the Bally club in Naperville. I was now the general manager and fitness director. I'd gone from affecting the people I was directly training to affecting all of those my trainers were training, too. I was given the responsibility not only for a small group of people but for everybody at the club. I was also having an effect on more than just fitness-minded people, more than just clients and trainers. I was working with the receptionist at the front desk, the maintenance guy, and the marketing people, too.

I believe this is what compelled me to study not only fitness but motivation as well. I was able to see my leadership and management style helping people in all kinds of different roles, which empowered me to say, "I know there is more for me to do."

About this time I decided to take a job with a bigger club in Chicago. It was a bold move. I was trying to expand my knowledge base and knew I would be able to affect more people than just personal trainers. It was my first step out the door, which allowed me to leave the Naperville club without really leaving Bally. I knew I would be able to do more if I was exposed to different departments. In fact, I did do more, even though I was only there for a short time. I did everything I could to revamp the group exercise program to align it with company policy, and I reorganized their filing system and spreadsheets so that when I left it was all put together for the next person.

This was my first step out of the box. I was learning to believe in myself. I needed to learn what I was really capable of, because deep down I wanted to open my own business. When I understood what I could really do, I saw I was capable of doing so much more. I wanted to do my own thing but had always been fearful of not being able to provide for my family. I didn't think I could do it unless I was in a structured corporate situation, but I was slowly learning I didn't really need that to lean on.

I think a lot of people are fearful of spreading their wings, of not only stepping outside the box but ultimately soaring above it. I know it's hard to take that risk—but it's worth it.

That move allowed me to at least test my wings. I was able to do a good job and learn things about myself, so when other doors opened, all I had to do was jump through.

> Within each of us is a hidden store of energy. Energy we can release to compete in the marathon of life. Within each of us is a hidden store of courage. Courage to give us the strength to face any challenge. Within each of us is a hidden store of determination. Determination to keep us in the race when all seems lost.
>
> Roger Dawson

TAKING FLIGHT

If you want to empower yourself to reach your full potential, you need to know the difference between your intrinsic and extrinsic motivators. What are your intrinsic motivators? Some examples might be the joy of developing a particular skill or having a sense of doing something morally right. Take a moment to think about those intrinsic motivators, and write down at least three of them here:

_____

_____

_____

Now consider your extrinsic motivators, those factors unrelated to the tasks you perform, such as money, recognition, or approval. In other words, things that encourage you to do something whether or not you enjoy it. List at least three of those external motivators here:

_____

_____

_____

Simply understanding and then identifying these motivators is empowering. The more intrinsically motivated you are overall, the closer you will be to achieving your dreams. You will be more willing and eager to try new things, learn new material, take new risks, and undergo the changes required for continued growth. Empowerment is really about fueling the energy that generates motivation, the energy you need to make things happen. It's about increasing your enthusiasm for life, turning your vitality up a notch. Who doesn't need to do that?

When you get right down to it, it's all about energy. Everything in life is about energy. Heat, light, and sound are all forms of energy. To empower yourself, you've got to increase your energy. Arthur Gueli, a crisis counselor and self-improvement expert, writes: "Next time you get the chance to observe a high achiever in action notice the high level of self motivation. For the most part, all successful people have tremendous drive, enthusiasm, and energy."

Where does that energy come from? "In part," writes Gueli, "a person's interest level in a specific subject or process can result in excitement, which increases energy." There you have it. Being intrinsically motivated will increase your energy. The more intrinsically motivated you are, the more energy you will have. "But that's not the whole story," adds Gueli. "In order to continue operating at peak effectiveness and increase energy, you have to rejuvenate yourself both mentally and physically every day."

Doesn't that make sense? It's all about balance. Being out of balance consumes energy rather than creates it. Being in balance gives you the energy to reach for the stars.

Total fitness is holistic. It requires a whole-life approach. Even when you are working on purpose, loving what you do, you can still overdo it. Gueli suggests that your life is comprised of five areas: production (work, studying), fitness (exercise and nutrition), spiritual, social, and mental relaxation time. "To increase energy," he writes, "you must exercise all five dimensions of your nature consistently, in a wise and balanced way.[32]

If you think about it, investing in the last four areas—physical, spiritual, social, and mental—helps you cultivate greater intrinsic motivation. When you take time to explore and nourish your well-being in these key areas, you are learning to operate on a more intrinsic level overall. Creating value and investing in your physical vitality, spirituality, relationships, and intellect, all work to put you in touch with who you are and what you choose to do, simply because they feed your body, spirit, soul, and mind. By intentionally creating space in your life for what truly empowers you, you create greater balance; and by creating balance, you create energy. It's a self-generating energizing process. The more energy you have, the more empowered you feel; and the more empowered you feel, the more energy you have.

How empowered are you? Which areas in your life are *fueling* and which are *consuming* your energy? Focus on what creates energy for you rather than depletes it, and you will find you are more empowered to step out and do those things you've always dreamed of but have never before dared to do.

---

32. This and the preceding three quotations are from Arthur Gueli, "Increase Your Energy," *SuccessMethods.org*, http://www.successmethods.org/increase-energy.html (accessed May 2009).

When you are empowered, you can be your best self in every area of your life, including your vocational role (your role as breadwinner, housewife, mother, father, student, and so forth). When you're performing at your best in this part of your life, you're achieving what I call *focused fitness*. Someone who has exemplified focused fitness in my life is an amazing athlete, artist, activist, and friend, Stacy Kvernmo. She showed up in my life unexpectedly, like the amazing tomato garden that one day just popped up in the backyard at my new house. She keeps me young and on my toes, stokes the fire that keeps me from quitting, and, most importantly, keeps me honest. Stacy is ten years younger than I am but in many ways far surpasses me with her wise old soul, and we have learned a great deal from each other. I asked her some questions about what focused fitness meant to her, and she responded as follows.

GUEST EXPERT MOTIV8N' MOMENT
FOCUSED FITNESS (VOCATION)

★ How do you define focused fitness?

1   Focused fitness is being empowered to put forth your best self in your vocational pursuits. That empowerment comes from opening yourself up to possibility and being motivated enough to strive for something beyond yourself.

★ What are the most important things you can do every day to stay focused?

2   Keep a positive attitude, even when things get tough. Stay cool. Stress equals lack of faith.

3   Take time for yourself. If you are too stressed, eventually you will crack.

4   Set your goals. And remind yourself that the journey is more important than the end result.

5 Plan. Failing to plan is planning to fail.

★ Give some examples of SMART goal prompts to stay focused.

6 Sign up for a specific event related to your goal. This creates a timeline and an image in your head of the end result, what you are working so hard for. It will keep you moving forward.

7 Write down some due dates. Get out your iCal, Outlook calendar, day planner, or whatever you plan to use, and set some mini deadlines between now and your final goal date. This will keep your progress in check and help you stay motivated.

8 Journal your progress. Better yet, blog it. If people can follow your posts, they tend to hold you more accountable for your progress. That sense of accountability can be empowering.

> Do your work with your whole heart, and you will succeed—there's so little competition.
>
> Elbert Hubbard

I love what Stacy said: "Empowerment comes from opening yourself up to possibility and being motivated enough to strive for something beyond yourself." Empowerment is all about the heart. Empowering yourself is simply a matter of (a) opening your heart to something bigger than yourself and (b) engaging your whole heart in pursuit of it.

Life coach Lisa Gates writes, "If I ask you what you want for your life, you will undoubtedly say, 'I want to make an impact, do something good. I want my life to matter.'" She adds that "to want something bigger than yourself means you want something big *for you*." And that's a good thing for everybody. Gates suggests that every student attending public school should be required to undergo what she calls "purpose training" because, she writes, "values, passion, and purpose give us the kind of flexibility we need to not only survive, but thrive in a world that changes constantly." Imagine growing up with this kind of empowerment. Imagine every high school graduate being issued a GED, or *Greater Empowerment Diploma*. Gates asks, "What would we do with a world full of clear-minded people who know their strengths and focus on them? Who are competent and practiced in making values-based choices? Who have as much mental and spiritual core strength as they do physical core strength? What would we do?"[33]

What would *you* do?

> He who loses himself in passion has lost less than he who loses his passion.
>
> Saint Augustine

---

33. This and the preceding three quotations are from Lisa Gates, "Our Young People Need Us to Want Something Big," *Craving Balance*, September 21, 2009, http://www.cravingbalance.com/craving-balance/2009/9/21/our-young-people-need-us-to-want-something-big.html (accessed April 18, 2009).

Every day, take a negative
and turn it into
a positive.

NEGATE THE NEGATIVES

CHAPTER 9

> Always turn a negative situation into a positive situation.
>
> Michael Jordan

You're on your way to developing the motivational STRENGTH that will see you through any challenge. You have taken the action steps of setting SMART goals, thinking about what you want, revving up your relationships, and empowering yourself. Next, I want to show you how to *negate the negatives.*

Negating the negatives will give you strength in the most challenging times. Never forget that strength is not defined by the absence of moments of weakness but by our ability to overcome in them. Strength of character, heart, mind, and soul comes from our intrinsic ability to find the positive in the weakness, to work through the negative experiences, and to become stronger because of them. It comes from doing what we think we can't do, or pressing through the resistance, whether it be our own fear or some misfortune.

When I left the Naperville club to work in Chicago, I had to overcome some resistance. Any change in direction, not to mention the challenge of taking on new responsibilities, can be unsettling. But in the same way a muscle grows stronger when it is pushed to its limits, so we grow through challenges. Working at the bigger club in the city gave me the opportunity to test my wings as a leader, and I grew from that.

Soon I was presented with another opportunity to grow. In fact, within only a month, I was offered a job managing a successful Italian restaurant in an affluent suburb. It paid twice as much as what I was making at Bally. Entirely motivated by this extrinsic reward, I took the job, but some serious negatives soon led me into a downward slide.

Interestingly, just prior to my taking the job, we hired a woman as a trainer at Bally who ran her own event-planning business. She was impressed with my teaching and motivational style and said she'd love to have me come speak at a women's luncheon. I was really excited to take that opportunity. I didn't prepare a PowerPoint presentation; I just spoke from my heart, and my message was well received. Here I was talking about taking responsibility for your actions—your destiny is not by chance but by choice; it's about learning from yourself and setting SMART goals—everything I teach about how to stay motivated. But I was thinking, *Wow. This is awesome. I love this stuff. Now why am I going to manage this Italian restaurant?*

I did start working at the restaurant, and I thought it was the best decision because the job offered a significantly larger salary. But guess what. I was miserable. I am naturally a hands-on, creative, take-charge kind of person. I thought I would be able to make improvements and indirectly transform lives in this management position. Not so. The owners were not interested in anything I had to say; there was absolutely no openness to change. Basically I was a figurehead who stood around in the back looking busy.

I was dying inside, wilting, and wondering how long I would be able to last. Just as I had known it was time for me to leave Blue Cross Blue Shield, I knew this job really wasn't for me. I was laid off after only a couple of months. The financial commitment to the management team seemed unrealistic in relation to projected profits, and not long after I was laid off most of the management was let go.

This was a difficult time for me personally, professionally, financially, and even physically. Although I hadn't been happy in that job, I felt I had let my family down, I had made a mistake, I was a loser, and there wasn't any future for me.

This was definitely a time of many negatives. I didn't understand what was going on. I had felt as though things were starting to turn around, and I was so excited about this new beginning. It didn't make sense to me that this could be happening. I didn't know what I would do. My husband was doing a part-time bartending job at night and staying home with the children during the day, allowing me to work and pursue my ambitions. (What a great guy!) But now I was desperate for rent money. Much to my chagrin, I had to ask my grandmother for a loan. With her help, we were able to get through the next couple of months. But during those two months, I hit my real low.

> Strength does not come from winning. Your struggles develop your strengths. When you go through hardships and decide not to surrender, that is strength.
>
> Arnold Schwarzenegger

UP, DOWN, AND BACK AROUND

Everything happens for a reason. We move through cycles of highs and lows, and ultimately what we thought was the worst possible thing ends up being to our advantage. In hindsight, pursuing the job at the restaurant was the final step I needed to venture out on my own. I was thankful for my past jobs and all of the opportunities they'd given me, but I was tethered to the concept of needing a corporate job with a regular salary and benefits. I couldn't think past this scenario even though I had dreamed of doing something on my own.

Though this low time was painful, I can now see its purpose. Because of what seemed like a fiasco at the time, I am doing the things I'm doing now, like writing this book. If we try, we can always find a way to turn a negative into a positive. According to Dr. Pamela McLean and Dr. Frederic Hudson, cofounders of the Hudson Institute, "Each new turning point in our lives offers us the invitation to examine our life priorities and assess what's most important for us to attend to at this particular junction in the journey."[34]

Hudson and McLean use what they call the cycle of renewal to describe the different life phases we are continually in the process of moving through. There are

---

34. Frederic Hudson and Pamela McLean, "Life Launch: A Passionate Guide to the Rest of Your Life," *The Hudson Institute of Santa Barbara*, http://www.hudsoninstitute.com/transition/lifelaunch/ (accessed April 15, 2009).

four distinct phases in the renewal cycle. Phase one is the "go for it" stage and represents commitment to positive goals. Phase two is appropriately called "the doldrums" because of the reactive, negative, and trapped feelings that predominate. Phase three is where feelings of depression can occur and is described as "cocooning," as we turn inward. This phase, however, gives way to self-reflection and tapping into core values, which causes us to explore, network, and train in the fourth and final phase, aptly called "getting ready." The fourth phase leads us back into the first phase, where we "go for it" once again, and the whole cycle starts over. This continuous cycle causes us to develop as individuals throughout life.[35]

Keeping in mind where you are in the process can help you stay a little more optimistic throughout those difficult phases. Each is like a season—winter, spring, summer, and fall—and you can settle into knowing "this too shall pass." The green foliage of summer always gives way to the leaves turning in fall, and the blanket of snow covering the bare branches of winter provides the cocoon for the buds of spring.

In his "Address Before the Wisconsin State Agricultural Society," delivered on September 30, 1859, Abraham Lincoln said:

> It is said an Eastern monarch once charged his wise men to invent him
> a sentence, to be ever in view, and which should be true and appropriate
> in all times and situations. They presented him the words: "And this,
> too, shall pass away." How much it expresses. How chastening in the
> hour of pride. How consoling in the depths of affliction.

There is something comforting about knowing that the season you're in is temporary and also that it is serving a purpose. King Solomon said, "To everything there is a season, a time for every purpose under heaven."[36] Even though the phase you're in now may look negative, you will see the positive results that will come because of it.

Your life may be in varying phases of growth. Your marriage might be stuck in "the doldrums," but you might be "getting ready" for the next chapter at your job and "going for it" in training for your next race. Understanding each phase is part of the growth process in and of itself. If you are "cocooning" in some area, you can know a new area of

---

35. Frederic Hudson and Pamela McLean, "Lifelaunch: Planning Your Next Chapter With Passion," *The Hudson Institute of Santa Barbara*, http://www.hudsoninstitute.com/pdf/lifelaunch.pdf (accessed May 2009).

36. *The New King James Version* (Nashville: Thomas Nelson, 1996), Ecclesiastes 3:1.

success is about to emerge. In the timeless words of Thomas Paine, "I love the man that can smile in trouble; that can gather strength from distress, and grow brave by reflection."

Going through the sometimes painful process of growth while being able to understand and embrace what was actually taking place has helped shape who I am today. The whole experience of losing my job at the restaurant after I had jumped the Bally ship brought me down off my pedestal and caused me to sit there dumbfounded on the floor for a while. I had to look deep inside myself and ask some hard questions. I suffered from depression, started drinking more heavily, and took an emotional time-out before I was able to snap out of it.

In fact, the restaurant experience took me completely around the renewal circle. When I first took the job, I was really excited. I was in phase one and ready to go for it. After a couple of months, I started feeling trapped. On the day I was laid off, I said to a coworker, "I don't know how long I can do this." I hadn't been allowed to express myself, and I really felt stuck. I think I had a sense that something else was coming around the corner, but I didn't know what to do about it. It was a gut feeling, an intrinsic urge I couldn't figure out at the time, but on a deep level it prepared me for what was about to happen. When the next thing did finally happen, I entered the painful but necessary cocooning phase. It provided the wake-up call I needed to enter the next phase of getting ready for the next chapter.

After two months of neglecting my health, putting on thirty pounds, and feeling like a complete louse, I decided to follow my own advice. I started working out again, cleaned up my diet, began networking, went back to school, learned some new things, and started talking about the book I wanted to write. I recruited clients, built my business as a fitness trainer, and started teaching classes and speaking wherever people were willing to listen to what I had to say. I began listening to myself, to all of the things I tell other people to do, and decided to be my own best student. It wasn't long before I was ready to go for it again.

In fact, things are going so well right now, I am a little worried because I know I am on my way around the circle again. But I am okay with that. And I am okay because

I know I can find strength in every weakness and turn every negative into a positive. You can, too.

> Our strength grows out of our weaknesses.
>
> Ralph Waldo Emerson

WHAT TO DO WHEN YOU'RE STUCK

Although negatives may be unavoidable in the various stages of growth, you can choose to be more intentional about transitioning through each phase by turning negatives into positives. The idea is to avoid getting stuck. You can use each phase to your advantage to prepare for the next. You can be more mindful and proactive as you understand where you are and identify what you need to do to move on. Even when you are at the height of going for it, knowing there will inevitably come a time when you will plateau and become discontent, you can brace yourself because you realize this is an expected, natural, even healthy part of the process of growth.

Each phase actually represents a new opportunity to check in with your intrinsic motivators. When you move from one phase to another, you are either moving closer to or further from what motivates you intrinsically. When you are going for it and begin to feel stuck, it's an indication that you are becoming decreasingly motivated on an intrinsic level. Then you have an opportunity to get back in touch with your true, inner desires, and as you do you will begin acting on those desires and getting ready for the next chapter.

When you feel stuck, take the opportunity to study yourself. Ask yourself, again and again if you have to, "What am I born to do? What am I passionate about?" This is exactly what cocooning allows you to do. It is a glorious time of turning inward and taking stock of what matters most to you and discovering what about you can benefit the world. It is an opportunity to reevaluate, adjust, or simply change your perspective and thoughts about yourself and your situation.

The key to controlling your life is to control your thoughts and reactions to the events of your life. Film producer Mike Todd said it like this: "I've never been poor, only broke. Being poor is a frame of mind. Being broke is only a temporary situation." It's all about seeing yourself on the other side of this situation. Losing your job (and even someone cutting you off in traffic) can throw you off balance, but you can navigate the negatives of any circumstance by staying focused on the positives—what gives your life meaning—in your present.

British actress Susan Hanson once mused, "What might my life be like were I to give in to the rhythms of my own ragged dance? Like this, I imagine . . . like this attentiveness, this pleasure, this being present to the world." Joy and meaning are always present, even in the ragged moments. It's something that comes from within. When we're in the difficult stages of life, changing our focus to that joy will carry us through till that moment when our potential emerges.

Finding joy in these times isn't easy. Our emotional state has a tendency to deteriorate when we are feeling stuck or turned inward for too long. Turning inward can be necessary and healthy, but what is helpful in small doses, like any medicine, can be destructive if not managed carefully. This is especially true when dealing with something as powerful as your emotions.

Your focus will determine whether or not your emotions work for or against you when you hit the rough times of transition. Business and leadership development specialist Tim Redmond states, "Choice is deliberate. Choice is a gift God gave us by which to create. . . . What are you focused on?" asks Redmond. "Your past? Your 'impossible' challenges? Your mistakes and regrets? Or your present possibilities? Your capacities? Your assets (especially relationships)?"[37]

Being proactive about what you focus on will determine how quickly you move from being stuck to going for it. What are some things you can do to change your focus? Well, you can start, as I did when I was in that negative phase, by setting SMART goals,

---

37. Tim Redmond, "Profitably Managing Your Emotional State," *Mastermind Club Newsletter*, February 20, 2009.

thinking about what you want, and revving up your relationships. By strengthening your connections with your purpose, passions, and other people, you direct your focus away from the negatives and toward positive solutions. In addition, focusing on the goals you want to achieve and the people you love reconnects you with your intrinsic motivators. And, as you know, the more intrinsically motivated you are, the more empowered you will be.

> We should not let our fears hold us back from pursuing our hopes.
>
> John F. Kennedy

PURSUE THE PATH OF POSSIBILITY

Overcoming negativity has been an important stage in my adult development. I learned the hard way that when we're extrinsically motivated *only*, we make mistakes. I left a great, albeit stressful, job at Bally for a complete career change to make more money for my family. But I also learned we can use those mistakes as springboards to propel us into something better, something intrinsically motivating that also includes the extrinsic rewards we are looking for.

My ever-faithful husband encouraged me to pursue my dreams of writing a book and opening my own business, dreams I had never considered realistic because I was always tethered to my idea of the perfect job. I had a book on my bedside table called *Smart Women Finish Rich* by David Bach. In the acknowledgment, Bach writes about his grandmother:

> Grandmother Bach once told me that the key to having a fulfilling life
> was to understand that life's greatest fruit was always at the end of the
> branch and that you had to be willing to fall out of the tree to get it.
> The key, I was told, was to have people around you who would catch
> you should you fall.[38]

---

38. David Bach, *Smart Women Finish Rich: 9 Steps to Achieving Financial Security and Funding Your Dreams* (Danvers, MA: Broadway Books, 1999), Acknowledgment.

I decided that with the support of my husband and best friends, I could reach for that dream and they would still be there for me if I fell. With their encouragement, I started writing, opened and marketed my personal training business, and started doing speaking engagements. As I continued networking and relationship building, I landed a book deal.

This positive change happened only because I had taken a risk and then had gone into, and more importantly, out of a period of depression. I found strength in my weakness by changing my focus and leaning on my family and friends. And even though my father and grandmother weren't with me, I relied on the strength they'd already instilled within me. I knew my father would have told me to push on. He would have said, "Onward and upward." And my grandmother would have told me, "Every kick is a boost."

The choices I make in my life are now centered on helping people. I want to show people that they can and will find strength in their weaknesses and, more importantly, that so many answers are right inside of them. We can all use our inner strength to make changes that will motivate and impact our lives and those of everyone around us.

I find satisfaction in my community involvement in creating an awareness of health and wellness. At the end of the day, I feel I've been most productive when I've seen a child's eyes light up or a mother who's lost a sense of who she is suddenly develop a bounce in her step. I also find solace in being a role model for my children. I see such possibility in them, in my clients, and in my community. I pursue this path with confidence that I can make an impact, knowing that's what gives my life meaning.

It's all about perspective. Maybe you're not feeling confident or seeing the meaning in where you are right now. There are so many ways you can reposition yourself on any given day to change your perspective and shed new light on your situation. Maybe you need a simple change of scenery. "I know you might think I'm crazy," said comedian Martin Lawrence. "I go into a different room, and I actually [feel] like it takes me to a better place, positive instead of negative."[39] Maybe you need to develop some new friendships or a new routine. Proactively seek a new outlook. Fifteenth-century scholar Desiderius Erasmus once said, "Give light, and the darkness will disappear of itself." You

---

39. Wilson Morales, "Bad Boys II: An Interview with Martin Lawrence," *BlackFilm.com*, July 2003, http://www.blackfilm.com/20030718/features/martinlawrence.shtml (accessed May 1, 2009).

can choose to take a negative and turn it into a positive and grow from the experience.

Motivational expert Josh Hinds observes that people interpret experiences differently. What one might see as negative, another will see as positive. "Basically, experiences are just that—experiences. It's the way we frame them that makes them either positive or negative." He also notes that "negative events tend to be more dense than positive ones. . . . Because negatives are more dense, or heavier in weight if you will, we notice them more than positive occurrences." With this in mind, Hinds suggests these six steps: "increase the amount of positive content you take in during the day"; "make an effort to expose yourself to positive people"; "take time to ponder the positive things you want to see occur in your life"; "track your positive achievements" in a journal; "review your personal success journal"; and "acknowledge that it's okay to have less-than-stellar days." [40]

I would add *acknowledge your weaknesses and how you've overcome them* and *take responsibility*. Remind yourself often that you are better and stronger because of the obstacles you've overcome. Be proactive about turning negatives into positives, redirecting your focus, and changing your perspective. How you frame your experience—and your destiny—is your choice.

Taking responsibility for your life and your outlook is one of the most positive and empowering things you can do.

> The instant we stop blaming, our negative emotions begin disappearing.
>
> Brian Tracy

MOTIV8N' SAM

A few weeks into my coaching journey with Sam, I observed how Sam's habit of focusing on the negatives, or always reacting negatively to certain things, sabotaged his best efforts to change. At first, this was difficult to get Sam to acknowledge.

---

40. This and the preceding two quotations are from Josh Hinds, "Changing Negatives to Positives," *Ezine @rticles*, http://ezinearticles.com/?Changing-Negatives-to-Positives&id=51679 (accessed May 7, 2009).

When Sam did become more aware of this tendency, he took the first step in turning it around. Once he began journaling his thoughts, I encouraged him to write down the things he felt were holding him back. He was always fully capable of turning a negative into a positive, or a weakness into a strength, but he had never slowed down enough to acknowledge it. By simply seeing some of these negatives in relation to his own personal power, Sam realized the negatives were diminishing.

For example, Sam does have a little bit of a temper and could easily let small things consume him. I asked him to start really looking at what made him angry or irritated. It could be anything from a malfunctioning cell phone to problems in his neighborhood to political issues he felt he had no control over. I told him to pay attention to whatever got him agitated, identify it, and then write it down. Over a period of two weeks, he logged everything he deemed negative, or that caused him to have a weak moment.

If we can identify what we consider to be problems, we will have more success in using them to strengthen rather than weaken us. Let me say here that identifying the negatives does not mean dwelling on them or thinking at length about all of the things you *don't* want to think about. Rather, it's simply becoming aware of them so you can start focusing on finding solutions and the positive outcomes you *do* want.

For example, if the exit you always take is clogged at the time you need it, use your GPS to find another route. Sometimes the answer is so simple.

In Sam's case, it was a matter of convincing him to not give up and succumb to the frustration. Once Sam was able to identify the individual issues he struggled with, he could then rework the problem, solve it, turn any of those negatives into positives, and see how his weaknesses could now become strengths.

> Every kick is a boost.
>
> Lawana Drown Berg

TURNING WEAKNESS INTO STRENGTH

I have another friend who is really an expert at turning weakness into strength. She has overcome incredible adversity, uses every challenge as a springboard for success, and has learned that every person has the innate power to create positive change in the world. Adrienne Hengels owns and operates Power of Your Om Yoga Studio in Naperville, Illinois. Why yoga? Adrienne believes yoga is about being true to your inner voice, being real, and truly living in the moment.

When Adrienne is not running her business or teaching yoga, she is training for long-course triathlons. She qualified for the 2009 Ironman World Championships in her first Ironman and has quickly become one of the country's fastest athletes in her age group. Through the combination of yoga and triathlons, Adrienne has learned that all things are possible if we stay emotionally fit by stepping outside our comfort zone, doubting our doubts, and truly believing we *are* capable. This is what I call *feeling fitness*. I wanted to get Adrienne's perspective on how to stay emotionally fit.

GUEST EXPERT MOTIV8N' MOMENT
FEELING FITNESS (EMOTIONS)

★ What is your definition of feeling fitness?

1   Feeling, or emotional, fitness is believing you have the power to achieve your goals, accepting that there will be challenges along the way that *could* hold you back, but making the conscious choice to rise above and take your journey one step at a time.

★ What are the most important things to do every day to become stronger in feeling fitness?

2 Laugh at yourself.

3 Accept that you are not your thoughts.

4 Do a little yoga every day. Even just twenty minutes will change your attitude, your body, and your life.

5 Embrace life's challenges and embrace change.

★ Give some examples of SMART feeling fitness goal prompts.

6 When setting a fitness goal for yourself, take it day by day or, at most, week by week. If you get caught up in the future, you will never accept what your body can do today.

7 When you have a setback, don't quit. Shake it off and begin again. Don't dwell on anything. Just accept it, learn from it, and start anew.

8 Make your health your number one priority. Just as you prioritize brushing your teeth and changing your underwear, plan your day in advance to be sure to get your exercise in. Don't give yourself the option to ever miss it. If you've planned your workout for after work, don't even *have* a conversation with yourself about how tired you are. Get your booty in the door and make it happen from there.

> Enlightenment—that magnificent escape from anguish and ignorance—never happens by accident. It results from the brave and sometimes lonely battle of one person against his own weaknesses.
>
> Bhikkhu Nyanasobhano

So get out there and "move it, move it." Strut your stuff. Make the most of what you have now and what you can do today. If you've got two arms and two legs, use them. Use whatever you have. Focus on what you *can* do. Play off your strengths even in the face of what seem to be your daunting weaknesses. Even the most skilled mountaineer scales the mountain one small step at a time. Strength training is simply a matter of increasing your ability to overcome resistance one tiny movement at a time—a movement that can sometimes be measured in inches. Focus on that one inch. You can move in any direction, achieve any goal, scale any mountain, one inch at a time. It's a matter of focus.

In the wise words of fashion icon Donna Karan, "Accent your positive and delete your negative." What Donna applies to wardrobe applies to life. Emphasize your assets. Focus on your strengths. Negate the negatives by magnifying the positives. "Once you replace negative thoughts with positive ones, you'll start having positive results," said the great Willie Nelson.

Think positively, speak positively, and pursue every action *expecting* a positive outcome. Yes, it is hard work, but you can do it. You can stay positive knowing every negative you overcome makes you stronger.

> The highest reward for man's toil is not what he gets for it, but what he becomes by it.
>
> John Ruskin

I can see the forest even through the trees
And if you want to, you also can believe.
Your mind will help you to achieve
everything your heart and soul can see.

It's about what you want out of life,

not about the woes, the trouble, and the strife.

It's the possibility and the dreams you need,

not the weakness that forces you down to your knees.

Pick a path, make a plan, check your route, take a stand.

You make the difference,

You take the chance,

You choose your life's experience.

Your heart and your soul are stronger than you knew,
So give in a little, take a breath, and let them guide you through.
Believe me when I say your journey's up to you . . .
To decide to be happy and, ultimately, to choose,

So now throw back your shoulders,

Stand proud and stand higher

You have arrived . . .

And now, bring your fire.

—Staci

It's not what you lift up.

It's whom.

GIVE BACK WITH GRATITUDE

Appreciation can make a day; even change a life. Your willingness to put it into words is all that is necessary.

Margaret Cousins

Staying strong and motivated is a challenge we all face. You've learned that to develop motivational STRENGTH, you need to set SMART goals, think about what you want, rev up your relationships, empower yourself, and negate the negatives. With your new focus on the positives, the next action step will be to *give back with gratitude*. Each of these steps will increase your motivation.

Even in the best of times, we can start focusing on the negatives and our motivation begins to wane. The key to sustaining motivational STRENGTH is to focus on the positives and to express gratitude for them. By acknowledging what is going right rather than wrong, and the goal rather than the obstacle, we channel our energies in the right direction.

Energy can be invested in either a productive or a counterproductive way. This applies not only to our personal lives but also to our communities. Are you showing gratitude for the gifts and strengths you have or regretting your own problems and weaknesses? Are you being a source of motivational STRENGTH to your organization, neighborhood, church, or school, or a demotivating squeaky wheel? Are you deficit-minded or asset-minded? Marian Wright Edelman, president and founder of the Children's Defense Fund, has said, "So often we dwell on the things that seem impossible rather than on the things that are possible. So often we are depressed by what remains to be done and forget to be thankful for all that has been done."

The idea of appreciating what works well and building on those strengths, rather than focusing on what doesn't work and compensating for weaknesses, is extremely powerful. David Cooperrider, who developed this revolutionary methodology for what he calls "organizational visions," established his own cycle of four processes, which include the following:

1   Discover the "best of what is" . . . .

2   Dream "what might be" . . . .

3   Design "what should be" . . . .

4   Create a Destiny based on "what will be". . . .[41]

You could almost take the four phases of the "renewal cycle" and turn them on their "organizational visions" head. If instead of focusing on the negatives in "the doldrums" phase you focused on what was working well, you could use as an opportunity to "discover" your strengths. You could use the self-reflection "cocooning" phase, during which you turn inward, as a time to "dream" and envision what would work well in the future. "Getting ready" could easily be translated into the planning process found in the "design" phase. And of course "go for it" and "create a destiny" both call for action toward your goals.

Instead of using classical intervention techniques when things aren't going well, such times could be seen as opportunities to discover, dream, and design new and better outcomes. "The arduous task of intervention will give way to the speed of imagination and innovation," states Cooperrider. "Instead of negation, criticism, and spiraling diagnosis, there will be discovery, dream, design, and destiny."[42]

What are you in the process of being grateful for? "Improving one's lot in life is a sign of health and growth," author Henry Miller once wrote. "But, we've got to be careful about always demanding some nonexistent perfection and learn instead to appreciate, to enhance what is in hand."[43] What you appreciate does appreciate; in other words, it increases in value. Author of the best-selling book *Codependent No More*,

---

41. Theodore Kinni, "The Art of Appreciative Inquiry," *Harvard Business School: Working Knowledge for Business Leaders*, September 22, 2003, http://hbswk.hbs.edu/archive/3684.html (accessed May 3, 2009).

42. David L. Cooperrider, Diana Whitney, Jacqueline M. Stavros, *Appreciative Inquiry Handbook for Leaders of Change*, 2nd edition (Brunswick, OH: Crown Custom Publishing; San Francisco: Berrett-Koehler Publishers, 2008), 2.

43. Henry Miller, edited by Frank L. Kersnowski and Alice Hughes, *Conversations With Henry Miller* (Jackson: University Press of Mississippi, 1994), 124.

Melanie Beattie, makes this amazing statement about the power of gratitude:

> Gratitude unlocks the fullness of life. It turns what we have into
> enough, and more. It turns denial into acceptance, chaos into order,
> confusion into clarity. . . . It turns problems into gifts, failures into
> success, the unexpected into perfect timing, and mistakes into
> important events. Gratitude makes sense of our past, brings peace for
> today, and creates a vision for tomorrow.[44]

Gratitude gives you the power to turn your negatives into positives. "Gratitude changes the pangs of memory into a tranquil joy," wrote Dietrich Bonhoeffer. It helps you to think about what you want, not what you don't want, by changing your focus from what is wrong to what is right. Your level of motivation on any given day is determined by your focus, and what you choose to focus on is simply an attitude. I've heard it said that your attitude determines your altitude, and your attitude is affected by your ability to appreciate the attributes and opportunities you've been given.

Aldous Huxley observed, "Most human beings have an almost infinite capacity for taking things for granted." This is why, I believe, most people struggle with staying motivated. If you want to transform your life, if you want to go to the next level, however you define it, then cultivate an attitude of gratitude.

> Gratefulness is the key to a happy life that we hold in our hands, because if we are not grateful, then no matter how much we have we will not be happy— because we will always want to have something else or something more.
>
> David Steindl-Rast

GRATITUDE THEORY UNVEILED

After conducting "The Research Project on Gratitude and Thanksgiving" at the

---

44. Melanie Beattie, *The Language of Letting Go* (Center City, MN: Hazelden Publishing, 1990), 218.

University of California, Davis, Dr. Michael McCullough and Dr. Robert Emmons discovered that gratitude plays a significant role in a person's sense of well-being. According to the ACF News Source, reporting for the *Osgood File*, "The results of the study indicated that daily gratitude exercises resulted in higher reported levels of alertness, enthusiasm, determination, optimism, and energy." The study observed three groups of people who kept daily journals. The first group simply recorded the events of the day, the second group recorded their unpleasant experiences, and the third group made a daily list of what they felt grateful for. "According to the findings, people who feel grateful are also more likely to feel loved. . . . Gratitude encouraged a positive cycle of reciprocal kindness among people since one act of gratitude encourages another."[45]

What has been discovered is that those who practice gratitude exercise more regularly, make more progress toward goals, are more focused, are more likely to help others, feel more connected, and have better attitudes toward their environment. Gratitude is a transformational force that can change lives. Yet while the study concluded that "grateful people report higher levels of positive emotions, life satisfaction, vitality, optimism, and lower levels of depression and stress," it also demonstrated that "grateful people do not deny or ignore the negative aspects of life, but they focus on the positive."[46] Grateful people are able to appreciate the lessons and unforeseen opportunities that negative events and experiences offer them.

How can you rewire your mind to operate from an attitude of gratitude regardless of your circumstances? Danea Horn suggests the answer lies in the subconscious mind. "It is the subconscious that controls much of our conscious experience," she states in her article "Gratitude Can Change Your Life." She argues that if you want a positive experience, you need a positive subconscious. "Hence, to make lasting change, we have to come at it from the subconscious mind—it needs reprogramming. This is where gratitude comes in." Horn proposes that the "easiest way to reprogram your subconscious is with gratitude because it is based on your current reality." It's just a matter of shifting your focus, but that shift goes beyond simple visualizations and daily affirmations. You have to *feel* as if you are already *experiencing* your desired outcome; otherwise, your

---

45. This and the preceding quotation are from "Gratitude Theory," *ACFnewsource*, http://www.acfnewsource.org/religion/gratitude_theory.html (accessed May 5, 2009).

46. This and the preceding quotation are from Robert A. Emmons, "Highlights from the Research Project on Gratitude and Thankfulness: Dimensions and Perspectives of Gratitude," *UC Davis Psychology*, http://psychology.ucdavis.edu/labs/emmons/ (accessed May 5, 2009).

subconscious will sabotage every conscious thought you are able to conjure up.

As you build up those feelings of gratitude, you begin to have outward experiences that support and create more feelings of gratitude because your subconscious will be acting from a place that believes you have a lot to be grateful for.[47]

Our outward experiences are so profoundly influenced by our inner feelings. When we're grateful, we negate the negatives and change our experience into a positive one.

> When you are grateful—when you can see what you have—you unlock blessings to flow in your life.
>
> Suze Orman

THE ENERGIZING POWER OF GRATITUDE

Physical energy really is a product of mental energy—more specifically, emotional energy. If you are not in a positive place emotionally, you probably won't be motivated to exercise or eat right. Motivational STRENGTH, therefore, is a product of positive energy. Gratitude creates positive energy and is an extremely revitalizing emotional force. An attitude of gratitude will lift your heart and add pep to your step. It will open your mind and heart to all of the good things at work in your life and give you reason to hope.

Hope and gratitude go hand in hand. Gratitude will foster hope, while being ungrateful will destroy it. As Melody Beattie has stated, "Gratitude makes sense of our past, brings peace for today, and creates a vision for tomorrow." If you are not grateful for where you've been and where you are now, you will not have any positive vision for the future. Practicing gratefulness will cause you to think about what you do want and not about what you don't want. It will nourish your relationships in amazing ways and transform the negatives of yesterday into the positive springboards of tomorrow.

---

47. This and the preceding three quotations are from Danea Horn, "Gratitude Can Change Your Life," *Ezine @rticles*, http://ezinearticles.com/?Gratitude-Can-Change-Your-Life&id=2217785 (accessed May 5, 2009).

"If you want to turn your life around," advises Gerald Good, "try thankfulness. It will change your life mightily."

Believe it or not, gratefulness will do more than turn your life around. It will do more than improve your outlook and increase your motivation. It will even do more than attract the opportunities and great outcomes you've always dreamed about. Studies show that expressing thanks will actually make you healthier and cause you to live longer. "Grateful people tend to be more optimistic, a characteristic that boosts the immune system and increases longevity," states Dr. Jan Garavaglia.[48]

What is it about gratitude that's so healthy? What does it do in the body exactly that strengthens the immune system? It has to do with how feelings of appreciation strengthen connections physiologically as well as socially. When you are thinking grateful thoughts, your body releases a neurotransmitter called acetylcholine, which slows down your heart rate and brings all of the functions of the body into alignment. Because of this calming effect, which is closely associated with oxytocin, you experience an increase in your capacity to be patient with others. Appreciation and gratitude are the primary catalysts for the release of the harmonizing hormone oxytocin and the good feelings it creates in the body—and for the harmony and good feelings created between people as a result.

Releasing the healing power of oxytocin has a great deal to do with your ability to get in touch with your intrinsic motivators. "When we're grateful, we recognize the intrinsic, beneficial value of the object (whether a person, being, thing, or condition); but even more fundamentally, we perceive an underlying connection between it and ourselves," writes William Young. "A feeling of benign belonging suffuses our gratitude. This feeling runs much deeper than a mere commerce of values, where the coin of exchange is only personal satisfaction." Young states that the healing power of gratefulness is its unifying force. It brings each individual into a place of feeling connected with the events and people around them, and it brings communities into a place of harmony as a result. Young explains, "We discover gratitude's healing power, seeing opportunity for growth in the midst of troubles, embracing the wisdom of beginnings and endings, and

---

48. Jan Garavaglia, "Longevity Rx," *Discovery Health*, http://health.discovery.com/centers/mental/longevity-rx.html (accessed May 7, 2009).

tolerating limitations while striving for better ways.[49]

Faith is really what's at the heart of gratitude. It takes a degree of faith to see past the problems and instead appreciate limitless potential. It requires that you continue to hope for what you can't yet see and that you love and appreciate what little you already have.

Studies show that grateful people do tend to be more spiritually aware and less materialistic and, as a result, suffer less anxiety about their personal performance, appearance, or economic status than their peers do. This decreases their bodies' production of the stress hormone cortisol, which is famous for suppressing the immune system. Simply put: If you want to boost your immunity, learn to count your blessings.

> Gratitude is a vaccine, an antitoxin, and an antiseptic.
>
> John Henry Jowett

PUTTING GRATITUDE INTO PRACTICE

While I was still teaching at the Hospital Corps School in Chicago, I had an opportunity to do a dramatic reading of Maya Angelou's "Phenomenal Woman" for Black History Month. This was another pivotal moment for me, because I wasn't just teaching something; I was expressing myself creatively. I saw I could touch people on the level of the heart and not just the head. Until then, I had only gotten up in front of people to teach first aid and CPR. This was the first time I spoke from my heart and was able to connect on a deeper level with my audience.

I loved this connectivity. It inspired me. I felt alive with gratitude for the experience, the people, and the poem. It energized me in a way I hadn't felt before. I was also moved by the gratitude of the audience.

I think of moments when I've felt I was giving something of myself, making a positive impact, feeling and giving appreciation. For every one of those opportunities I

---

49   This and the preceding two quotations are from William Young, "The Healing Power of Gratitude," *Gratefulness.org*, http://www.gratefulness.org/qbox/item.cfm?qbox_id=63 (accessed May 1, 2009).

am grateful. I am thankful for my relationship with God, because I don't think I would be where I am without Him in my life, and I couldn't keep moving forward without knowing He is with me all the time. I am grateful for what my father taught me and for my relationship with my grandmother. I am thankful for the opportunity to do work I love, for my clients, and for how I've been able to impact their lives. It's priceless when someone thanks me for empowering them to improve their health. I am so thankful for being able to help young people change their path and become focused and stay focused. I am so grateful for the connections I have with my friends. I am thankful to my stepmother for teaching me the definition of *resilience*. Of course, I could go on . . . and on . . . and on, but I want to ask you: What are you grateful for?

It is so important to count your blessings. Take time to write them down. It is surprisingly healing, restorative, and rejuvenating. It has taken me a long time to come to the place where I can take every negative thing in my life and truly appreciate it. At one time, I had to force myself to be grateful for what I did have: my family, my health, my experiences, and my infinite opportunities. When I was able to appreciate what I had in my hand at the time, I started doing a lot of writing. Appreciating what I did have stirred up my hope, and I began preparing for speaking engagements as though I already had them lined up. I changed my focus to gratitude, and things started falling together. Opportunities began presenting themselves, clients started coming, and somehow I built the momentum I needed to go back to school. Since that time, I have been doing consulting, developing corporate wellness clients, expanding my personal training base, and working with the Miss Illinois organization as their primary coach and trainer.

When you take time to reflect on the blessings in your life, you'll automatically begin to draw more blessings to yourself. You create what you focus on.

LEARNING TO WITNESS THE FITNESS

As I've mentioned, grateful people are more spiritually aware. Gratitude and spiritual fitness are interconnected. I like to refer to spiritual fitness as *witness the fitness*. I learned so much about the beauty and spiritual power of gratitude from Pastor Dave Ferguson at Community Christian Church in Naperville, Illinois. As the past year has brought me through an extensive journey of personal growth, I am very grateful for the opportunity to find someone like Dave to help me understand and implement the "attitude of gratitude." The tips below were inspired by the experiences and lessons I learned from him.

GUEST EXPERT MOTIV8N' MOMENT
WITNESS THE FITNESS (GRATITUDE)

★ How can someone know they are "fit" in the area of gratitude?

1 Being grateful is not just saying "thank you." It's a lifestyle. It means you don't take for granted life's little miracles. Gratefulness permeates your thoughts, expressions, objective and subjective interactions with others, and, more importantly, how you act when no one is watching.

★ What are the most important things to do every day to become more grateful?

2 The obvious is to actually say "thank you"—and mean it.

3 Take stock in what you have that you are grateful for. Make sure you appreciate it on a daily basis.

4 Journal attitudes of gratitude you may not be ready to verbalize. This will help you identify your emotion behind it.

5 Start paying attention when people thank you for something. Take a moment to notice how it feels; then pass that feeling on.

★ What are some examples of SMART goal prompts to strengthen an attitude of gratitude?

6 Find someone you *know* you should show gratitude toward but don't. Then do!

7 Journal your thoughts on what you are grateful for, followed by why you think you've had trouble expressing it.

8 Shower gratitude on someone and see what happens. Write a letter, send a gift, and follow up with a phone call or personal conversation. Take note of how *you* feel afterward. Remember those feelings and go back to them. Your feelings and emotions are powerful connectors to future positive behaviors.

> If the only prayer you said in your whole life was, "thank you," that would suffice.
>
> Eckhart von Hochheim

EXERCISE (AS IN, DO) THANKFULNESS

Gratitude can be hard to foster when we are experiencing problems. Maybe you've just lost your job, or you're not making ends meet, or you're struggling in some other way. Maybe everything in your life isn't the way you want it to be, but you have to admit, there are some things that are good. If you can maintain focus on the things going well and appreciate, and then maximize, the opportunities you've been given, I promise things will get better.

Joseph Mercola discusses the value of gratitude when it comes to keeping your job. He writes, "Believe it or not, looking on the bright side of things can be good for your career and your mental health. Research shows that an attitude of gratitude in trying times can not only help you keep your job, but get you the job you want."[50] Mercola reports that workers who add positive energy, rather than negative energy, to their workplaces are most likely to experience job security.

---

50. Joseph Mercola, "If You Want to Keep Your Job, Be Happy," *Mercola.com*, April 28, 2009, http://articles.mercola.com/sites/articles/archive/2009/04/28/if-you-want-to-keep-your-job-be-happy.aspx (accessed May 1, 2009).

So what does this mean for you and me? We need to practice the art of gratefulness. We need to cultivate an attitude of gratitude, but more than that, we must *show* appreciation. In the words of inspirational author William Arthur Ward, "Feeling gratitude and not expressing it is like wrapping a present and not giving it." We must be proactive about expressing gratitude.

Yet, as John F. Kennedy noted, "As we express our gratitude, we must never forget that the highest appreciation is not to utter words, but to live by them." Giving back with gratitude is a lifestyle choice. It is how we choose to live and what we *do* that count. "To speak gratitude is courteous and pleasant, to enact gratitude is generous and noble, but to live gratitude is to touch Heaven," wrote the poet and theologian Johannes A. Gaertner. How can you live gratitude today?

> Gratitude is something of which none of us can give too much. For on the smiles, the thanks we give, our little gestures of appreciation, our neighbors build their philosophy of life.
>
> A.J. Cronin

Motiv8n' Sam

Interestingly, Sam thought, as many of us do, that we show our gratitude simply by feeling it. I asked him to take notice of when he actually *said* "thank you" each day. He told me he always *felt* thankful and grateful, but when it came down to it, he didn't actually say it.

When Sam said this, I had to ask myself how often *I* actually showed or spoke my gratitude every day. Sam hadn't heard me express my gratitude very often. It is an easy thing to take for granted. Even though I was the one explaining the importance of verbally showing gratitude, I had neglected it myself. It is humbling and important to be given those reality checks now and again. Thanks, Sam.

> I would maintain that thanks are the highest form of thought; and that gratitude is happiness doubled by wonder.

G.K. Chesterton

Use It or Lose It

So how can you begin infusing your life with the abundance a grateful heart provides? Start by taking a moment to appreciate your own body. Calm your mind, breathe in deeply, and think about how wonderful it is just to be able to breathe. Ah, now doesn't that feel good? On your next inhale, slowly count to eight while you breathe in, and then breathe out slowly for another count of eight. When you have settled into the rhythm of deep breathing, say to yourself on your next inhale, *I am so blessed.* As you slowly exhale, say to yourself, *I am so grateful.* Repeat for eight breaths. Notice how energized and positive you feel now.

The next thing I would suggest you do is record what you are grateful for. Take a few minutes at the end of each day to write down eight things you are thankful for. What did you appreciate learning? How did someone bless you? How did an event unfold to work in your favor?

List 8 things you are grateful for:

_____

_____

_____

_____

_____

_____

_____

_____

List 8 people you are thankful for and why:

_____

_____

_____

_____

_____

_____

_____

This leads to the next exercise you can put into practice every day. Don't let a single day go by without sending a note of thanks to *someone*. It doesn't have to be fancy. It could be a quick postcard or an e-mail or text or phone call with a few words expressing your gratitude. You can Twitter or Facebook your thanks. Just make sure you acknowledge someone each day with your appreciation for them. More than anything else, people are the gifts we've been given to bring joy and meaning to our lives and help us become the best we can be.

> The unthankful heart . . . discovers no mercies; but let the thankful heart sweep through the day and, as the magnet finds the iron, so it will find, in every hour, some heavenly blessings.
>
> Henry Ward Beecher

8 HEALTHY OPTIONS I'M REALLY GRATEFUL FOR

1 Bragg Apple Cider Vinegar

2 Easy-to-eat veggies. Bag up single portions of raw veggies for a grab-and-go healthy snack. Try mixing three or four at a time, such as baby carrots, sugar snap peas, sliced peppers, broccoli, cauliflower, celery, cherry tomatoes, green beans— you get the idea!

3 The George Foreman Grill. Don't even get me started!

4 The amazing sweet potato. Can be cooked for four minutes in the microwave, or to maximize nutritional integrity, bake in the oven for forty minutes.

5 Egg whites. Massive protein punch without the fat and calories. Can also be cooked in the microwave, and great with salsa and broccoli mixed in.

6 Ezekiel bread (and steel-cut oats in bulk). Both great sources of fiber *and* protein.

7 Lean ground turkey. Great protein source for those tired of chicken. Brown with veggies, or mix in salsa. Yummy!

8 Every antioxidant-packed fruit—berries, apples, grapefruits, melons, etc.

*Your successes are in
direct proportion to
your efforts.*

TAKE CHARGE

> We must look for ways to be an active force in our own lives. We must take charge of our own destinies, design a life of substance, and truly begin to live our dreams.
>
> Les Brown

You've been setting SMART goals, thinking about what you want, revving up your relationships, empowering yourself, negating the negatives, and giving back with gratitude. Now it's time to take the next action step to develop motivational STRENGTH. It's time to *take charge*.

To take charge of your dreams, you must already be empowered. As you've seen, empowerment comes when you are able to turn your negatives into positives and appreciate what motivates you intrinsically. Tapping into your intrinsic motivators empowers you to move through the times you are stuck and withdrawn into times of anticipation and "activation"—the "go for it" and "deliver" phases we talked about. An attitude of gratitude can help you connect and cultivate what has intrinsic value to you, largely by connecting you with other people and a higher purpose. Practicing gratefulness causes you to think beyond your own selfish desires and, well, grow up. It creates a certain maturity that gives you the confidence to move forward. It endows you with the wisdom you need to see the bigger picture and focus on what matters most. Until you have an attitude of gratitude, you won't have the inner confidence required to take charge of your life.

Your ability to take charge comes from confidence; it comes from within. You can fuel confidence by taking charge of your own attitude. Actively giving of yourself with gratitude rather than passively taking others for granted will give you the self-control you need to take command of your destiny. Irish playwright George Bernard Shaw wrote, "This is the joy of life: the being used up for a purpose recognized by yourself as a mighty one; being a force of nature instead of a feverish, selfish, little clot of ailments and grievances, complaining that the world will not devote itself to making you happy." I love that! It's really about how you position yourself in the world, as a giver or a taker. This stance will ultimately determine whether you *make* things happen or just *let* them happen.

It's been said, "Take charge of your attitude. Don't let someone else choose it for you." The key to getting your body and life in shape and keeping them that way is learning to manage your attitude, no matter where you are in the renewal cycle. Until you do, you'll never be in charge of your life. Someone or something else always will be. "We can let circumstances rule us," said motivational pioneer Earl Nightingale, "or we can take charge and rule our lives from within." The degree to which you are able to rule from within will determine your capacity to manage change and rule your outer world.

When I made a choice to rule my life from within, I put my current situation and experiences to work for me. If nothing else, I had time. I stopped *spending* time and started *investing* it. Appreciating the gifts and opportunities I already had helped me take charge of my life. For me, as a fitness instructor and motivational enthusiast, this meant building my own training business, preparing better presentations for bigger audiences, entering two fitness competitions—Bikini Universe and the Mid-Illinois Bodybuilding and Figure Championship—and getting this book together.

> Have a purpose in life, and having it, throw such strength of mind and muscle into your work as God has given you.
>
> Thomas Carlyle

Going for It

When you go for it, you decide you are your own person. You really take charge of who you are, who you want to be, and what you want to represent. It's easy to blame others for where we are, and it's easy to excuse our bad behaviors by saying we're just being who we are. Instead, we have to choose to take responsibility for where we are and then choose to take charge by stepping toward our goals.

Taking charge requires committing to personal integrity. It isn't about taking charge of a job or a situation or a family. It is more than that. It is being true to yourself, setting your course to follow your own North Star. You have to take charge of the direction you're headed. You might not know exactly where you'll end up, but you've got some kind of map in your hand, you're saddled up and ready to ride, and for the most part you like the horse you're on. More than that, you're grateful for it.

Being grateful opens you up to receive from others. It allows you to acknowledge other people's roles in the process so you can humble yourself enough to benefit from them. I wouldn't be where I am today if it weren't for my husband, friends, mentors, and clients. Because of their help and encouragement, I was able to do what I needed to take charge of my life. I listened to their advice and graciously received their help, and because of their presence and support I felt I could do anything. I like what psychologist Marilyn Barrick says: "For the most part, fear is nothing but an illusion. When you share it with someone else, it tends to disappear." That is the truth.

> Your life is the sum result of all the choices you make, both consciously and unconsciously. If you can control the process of choosing, you can take control of all aspects of your life. You can find the freedom that comes from being in charge of yourself.
>
> Robert F. Bennett

Being My Best

After having my second child in December of 2005 and quickly getting back into shape, I was asked by women everywhere at Bally, "What are you doing? What's going on? Your body looks fantastic." It was at this point that I almost felt obligated to go for it when it came to training and competing. For me, it was about more than just looking good; it was about challenging myself to be my best. If I was going to look good, I wanted to turn that into working really hard, challenging myself to achieve yet another goal so I could make it worth something. I didn't just want to walk around and look nice in a pair of shorts. I wanted to be able to say, "Here are some tangible things I did to look this way that made me feel better about myself and allowed me to learn so I would have something to give back." Partly I was investing in myself, but at the same time, I knew that by challenging myself and pushing the envelope, so to speak, I would be able to invest more in others.

I had become close friends with a seasoned competitor, Stacy Kvernmo, whom I introduced to you earlier in the book. She is ten years younger than I am, but we are so compatible, have the same sense of humor, and are the very best of friends. We call ourselves the Chicago Stacies.

In September of 2006 Stacy and I started training and working out together to prepare for the Mid-Illinois Bodybuilding and Figure Competition to take place in March of 2007. She won first runner-up in the tall division, and I won first runner-up in the short division. In June we headed to Miami for the Universe competition, where I won first runner-up in Bikini Universe and she placed fourth in Fitness Universe and ninth overall. Because of her friendship and example, I was able to step out and take charge of my life, and really my destiny, in a profound way.

Training and dieting were part of a massive learning experience, and I loved it. Training for a competition is completely different from training for everyday health and fitness. So much more goes into it. Of course, consistency and discipline are of paramount importance. Clean eating and diet are huge. I learned so much during this time when I took charge and decided to compete. My ability to help my clients take charge catapulted to a new level. I was named N.Y. Strength Fitness Director of the Year in 2007, and by the fall of 2008 I was training Miss Illinois as she prepared for the Miss America Pageant. I am now the official trainer for the Miss Illinois Organization and have absolutely loved helping these young women take charge of their lives.

> If we all did the things we are capable of doing we would literally astound ourselves.
>
> Thomas Edison

FEEDING THE POWER WITHIN

The first step in taking charge of your body is monitoring what goes *in* your body. To be quite honest, it wasn't until I trained for competition that I realized what clean eating meant to the achievement of goals, no matter what fitness level you are striving for. Every aspect of health and fitness is primarily diet-related; anything else you do in terms of exercise is secondary. I learned how simple carbohydrates affect your body and how processed food can deteriorate your health. I tell every single one of my clients to read *The Eat Clean Diet* by Tosca Reno. The information in her book is a key component of my consulting.

Actually, Tosca Reno is a great example of someone who took charge and turned her life around. She was at one of the lowest points in her life when she was forty years old. She weighed over two hundred pounds, was stuck in an unhappy marriage, and felt utterly disappointed with how her life had turned out. Her self-esteem was at an all-time low and "she barely recognized the woman she had become," says her Web site. Her online bio is inspiring.

Determined to change her life for the better, she entered the doors of her local gym and never looked back. The minute she hopped on the treadmill she felt like she was taking control of her life again. Her confidence grew as she found the motivation to take care of herself—something she had lacked for years. After learning how to Eat Clean, Tosca's life accelerated to new heights of health, vitality and confidence.[51]

Reno now has an entire line of diet and fitness books. I encourage you to visit her Web site (www.toscareno.com) and read her books.

I also wholeheartedly recommend Dr. Jack Barnathan's book *Precision Cuisine.* Dr. Jack talks about the quality of your food and what it means to the quality of your life. For example, don't be a bottom-feeder, eating a piece of tilapia. If you want to possess the fight it takes to go against the current, eat wild North Atlantic salmon, a fish that swims upstream fighting for its life. Eat bison instead of cow. It's all about the quality of the food instead of quantity, about intrinsic versus extrinsic value. It's what Dr. Jack calls "authentic nutrition." This is how he explains it on his Web site:

When a product or person is "authentic," we view them as "real." Something we can trust or made of ingredients that are true.

When it comes to food, this is evident in the texture, aroma, and remarkable way in which flavors are revealed to us. Sadly, if we've been conditioned to foods with preservatives like high fructose corn syrup and trans fats, we may never experience the authentic nature of food . . .

During my recent visit to Europe for my grandmother's ninetieth birthday, the difference was shocking. French Brie with flavors so rich it has ruined the American homogenized, bland-as-plastic version forever.

German grain breads with real grains throughout the bread bursting with flavor, not just sprinkled on top of the loaf for little more than looks.

Even the coffee is roasted in a manner that there is, as the waiter at a sidewalk café described to me, a "natural" foam of coffee goodness

51. Tosca's Biography," *ToscaReno.com,* http://www.toscareno.com/index.php?option=com_content&view=article&id=48&Itemid=54 (accessed June 4, 2010).

swirling at the top when poured into a cup. Authentic indeed.[52]

When food is authentic, it is so satisfying, rich, and flavorful that you are *not* left wanting more. Imagine that. This is the primary focus of Dr. Jack's and Tosca Reno's philosophies. Quality over quantity. Intrinsic over extrinsic. In other words, how close to its original source is the food you are eating? Or are you eating only what looks good, is packaged well, or is convenient? I encourage you to sign up for Dr. Jack's online magazine and download a copy of his book at his Web site. The more you know about what you're eating, the better you will eat—and the better you will feel. In this case, knowledge truly is power: a powerful health tool you can't afford to live without. You might be able to exist without it, but you won't be living the kind of life that being fit and feeling fabulous offer you.

If you don't want to live like a bottom-feeder, why eat like one? I think of it as getting past those bottom three layers on Maslow's Hierarchy of Needs, going against the current and pushing your way upstream to the top two tiers. Work on improving your self-esteem, tap into your intrinsic motivators, and empower yourself by living and eating authentically. Push past extrinsic, superficial, materialistic, and quantity-over-quality goals. You'll get to the place where purity, authenticity, and deep intrinsic motivations define you. To me, this is what it means to take charge.

Taking charge will require you to go against the currents of the status-quo tides in your life. It will mean embracing changes and challenges, taking risks, and doing things you're not used to or have never done before. "It is important to remember," said Max Dupree, "that we cannot become what we need to be by remaining what we are." If you are to take charge of your life, you can't have a "go with the flow," "wait and see what happens," "eat whatever comes my way" attitude. Motivational columnist Martin Woolnough writes: "It can be hard to buck the flow, to go against the trends, but at times this is what is needed. Otherwise we can end up on the losing end of things. Little by little things slip, in one area, then another. Little by little we lose a little something of ourselves." He goes on to talk about something very similar to the renewal cycle:

---

52. Jack Barnathan, "Mercury in Your Meal—or Authentic Food?" *PrecisionCuisine.com*, http://precisioncuisine.com/id7.html (accessed May 7, 2009).

A temporary "injunction" may occur where we start to take stock. Assess what we are doing. Realize what is happening. Look around us and see the effects of our inaction. How our lack of taking responsibility for ourselves affects our actions.

Life has this habit of rebounding and catching us unawares, as if to teach us a lesson. At those moments, in those situations, at those times we need to stand up and be counted. . . . We need to understand that something has to change. We have to change.

These are the moments when we are forced to wake up and take charge, or else go back to sleep. Woolnough concludes, "It is so much better to be up front and be responsible for the things we do, for our thoughts, for our actions, for our deeds"[53]—and I would add for our diet. When you wake up and take charge, you change the trajectory of your life; you turn the tide of your destiny.

Think of Tosca Reno. She could have stayed where she was, in her unhappy relationship, overweight, and living every day as she had lived the day before. She instead chose to paddle against the current and swim upstream by pulling on the lifeline of her intrinsic motivators. She also caught hold of the life preserver called "eating clean."

You are never too old to grab onto your intrinsic motivators and that clean-food life preserver. In fact, there is something to be said for those of us who are older and wiser. I see the women competitors my age and older who are able to embrace their whole authentic self, both their strengths and their weaknesses, laugh at their shortcomings, and truly appreciate having overcome something (such as the effects of time). They have inner 'tude that says, "I am fine because I have been refined." You can see it. Often the winners are not the younger girls with the better bodies but the older, more confident women. This confidence radiates strength and beauty from the inside out.

This kind of strength and fitness is rooted in authenticity. It is reflected, or perhaps fueled, by the food you eat. You must eat authentic food to achieve authentic strength. When you tune up an instrument, you make sure everything works in harmony. The

53   This and the preceding two quotations are from Martin Woolnough, "Don't Pass the Buck—Take Responsibility for Your Life," *Articlesbase.com*, http://www.articlesbase.com/motivational-articles/dont-pass-the-buck-take-responsibility-for-your-life-669511.html (accessed May 9, 2009).

same is true of you; you have to tune up every dimension of yourself—spirit, soul, and body—to achieve harmony. Similarly, when you're tuning up an engine, you pay special attention to what you put into it. You must also pay attention to what you put into yourself: from what you think to what you eat.

> Tell me what you eat, and I will tell you what you are.
>
> Anthelme Brillat-Savarin

I want to reintroduce the amazing Dr. Jack Barnathan. Dr. Jack came into my life about nine years ago as my teacher and mentor. Now he is more like a father to me. He took me under his wing and then taught me how to soar. He always believed in the potential I had buried inside me, and to tell you the truth, he was relentless about not ever letting me forget it. He possesses an astounding wealth of knowledge in the areas of health, wellness, and fitness. As a doctor of chiropractic medicine, he is able to combine all of these disciplines to present industry-changing concepts. I am honored by his mentoring all of these years and give major credit for my successes to this great man. As my guest expert on nutritional fitness, he shares his valuable insights on feeding your fitness below.

GUEST EXPERT MOTIV8N' MOMENT
FEEDING YOUR FITNESS (NUTRITION)

★ What is feeding your fitness, or nutritional fitness?

1 Quality life is the result of consistent choices that support growth and happiness. Choose to transform every meal into a healthy and meaningful one you remember.

Life is nothing without meaning, and you must translate this into your relationship with food. Feeding your fitness, or being nutritionally fit, means having a healthy, quality relationship with wholesome, authentic food.

★ What are the most important things to do every day to feed your fitness?

2   First, examine the quality of your food. Why is it good for you? Learn why salmon is better for you than catfish, or why grass-fed beef is better than grain-fed.

3   Identify the "strength" in your food, such as the strength developed in the muscles of a bison, for example. You can't raise them in a pen like cows; they'll jump over or run right through it. Farm-raised salmon are stagnant and don't have to hunt for food, while wild salmon have to swim upstream and fight for their lives.

4   Focus on eating "clean" foods, such as organically grown (or raised) vegetables, fruits, beans, nuts, grains, fish, lean meats, and poultry.

5   Make it a priority to avoid all processed, packaged, pre-prepared foods, including all "fast foods" and "fast drinks" (such as soft drinks, energy drinks, juice drinks, or any artificially flavored drink).

6   Find the essence in the food you eat. The essence, or *terroir*, is derived from the soil an item or a person was raised in. More than taste, it is the heritage and hearth together. It is the true flavor of the food based on the land it was grown in. Understand how this essence affects the foods you eat. Develop a deeper, more meaningful relationship with your daily diet.

★ List some SMART goals for feeding your fitness.

7   Eat fit foods. Instead of a résumé of fat, carbs, and protein, you must find compelling reasons to fully, enthusiastically, even passionately, feel happiness when biting into wild Alaskan salmon steak.

8   Eat antioxidant rich foods. One of the most important benefits of antioxidants is that they counteract cortisol damage to brain cells and potentially protect function, such as memory.

STAYING ENGAGED

Your intrinsic motivation will keep you disciplined and consistent. If you have support from your loved ones, you can overcome setbacks, even irritability. When I was training, I probably wasn't the easiest person to be around because I wasn't eating a lot of carbs, and that will make anyone cranky. I was working out constantly and still trying to be a good manager, wife, and mother. My attention was divided because I was actually paying some attention to myself.

This was a turning point for me. Trying to work myself into my own life was a challenge. The time required to train was one thing, but the dieting part of it was really, really difficult. I was determined to set an example for women my age who have children, though. I wanted to do a good job and show discipline and consistency because it is something I speak about.

I'm not sure I would compete again because it's not worth the crankiness my husband and children had to suffer through. I'm also hesitant about competing again because of how I felt afterward. On one hand, it was awesome to have attained my goal and to have actually achieved runner-up; but on the other hand, I was left with some potentially unrealistic expectations. Here I was looking better than I have in my whole life, but I can't stay one hundred fourteen pounds forever. I struggled with that. I didn't like feeling that if I couldn't stay "show ready" I was no longer good enough. I didn't want to create a situation where I felt bad about myself, even though I was thrilled with what I had accomplished.

Yes, I was able to take charge and do it, but I can also take charge by saying, "You know, I don't need to keep doing it." I am motivated by what I'm involved in now. It's not about me. It's about the young women and clients I am training; it's about the people I'm helping through my work with a great youth mentoring program called Triple Threat Mentoring. I am still going for it, but what I'm doing to take charge of my life now is different from how I took charge before. I'm stepping out and challenging myself in different ways, but I am still engaging, exploring, and learning—and loving the journey.

The important thing for me is to be a good role model and leader. I don't need to be one hundred fourteen pounds and ready to walk onstage in a bikini every day to do that. But I can say I've done it. If you want to challenge yourself to do a fitness competition or triathlon, or run a marathon so you can say you've done it, go for it! You will learn and grow because of it. You will break through barriers and never be the same as a result. Give yourself that opportunity.

I think of it as having two paths in front of you where one engages you and the other disengages you. If you do something because it's an inspiring challenge and it causes you to feel as if you are taking charge of your life in a positive way, then it is an engaging goal for you. But when you stop to ask yourself whether your goal is engaging or disengaging and you become negative, then it might be the wrong path. The key is staying engaged.

When you are on that path of engagement, you will have limitless energy and stamina. You will have the motivational STRENGTH you need to stay the course. Part of staying engaged and maintaining energy is eating clean. When you are eating clean, authentic foods, you develop the inner strength that will arouse you to take charge. The food you eat is a source of energy, as are the thoughts you think, the words you speak, and the things you do.

Remember the definition of *motivation* from the opening pages of this book? "The psychological feature that arouses an organism to action toward a desired goal." This arousal, or energy, will motivate you to do whatever is necessary to achieve your desired goal. It's all about energy. Everything in life is about energy. Empowerment is creating the impulse and energy required to generate and sustain your motivational STRENGTH. To increase your strength, you've got to increase your energy. Fortunately, you are your own source of renewable energy. All you need to do is get in motion. "There's no secret to getting started," writes fitness expert Tom Venuto. "You simply decide and then take your first step. With each subsequent step, the next one becomes easier."

All we need to do is get moving. When you use energy at the gym or doing your favorite workout, it pumps you with energy. So get in motion. You have two sources of life-transforming energy—clean foods and exercise—which will boost your ability to take charge of your life.

What will you take charge of? Is it a onetime thing or an ongoing habit? Continuing to run marathon after marathon may not be the healthiest thing for *you*. Really think about whether or not what you are taking charge of is realistic. Does it lead you back to SMART goals? If you decide on an area or outcome you will take charge of, make sure it's definable. Can you break down what you are taking charge of into a specific, measurable, attainable, realistic, time-bound format? Decide at the outset if this will be a onetime challenge you want to achieve and, if so, whether you will be satisfied doing it just once. Think about what you want to achieve and why.

> If you are serious about your goals, drop the conditions. Go directly to your goal. Be your goal. Conditions often disguise strategies for escaping accountability. Why not just take charge and create the experience you are looking for?
>
> Eric Allenbaugh

MOTIV8N' SAM

From the beginning, Sam was great at taking charge of some major things. He totally cleaned his closet and garage and got started with configuring his budget and looking into retirement and savings. I was really proud of how he was able to discipline himself to follow the diet and exercise plan. However, Sam needed some extra "coaching" before he felt empowered enough to take charge of journaling his emotions. This was one area he really wanted to brush past. He used his journal only sporadically, and we ended up talking about this one little issue a lot. Finally, I had to get really firm with him and tell him I planned to check this journal every Tuesday when we had our coaching session.

Instead of forcing him to write down lengthy descriptions of his day, however, I told him all I wanted was one word. I said, "Sam, just write down one word each day to describe how you feel." I asked him to start with this one small step and then take it from there. And you know what? It worked. It was just enough for him to manage. He started the journaling process in earnest after this, and it has really helped him connect the dots as he's moved through some difficult situations and achieved some major milestones. It has helped him clarify his emotional triggers and stumbling blocks, as well as his strengths.

Through trial and error, lots of self-forgiveness, relentless communication, setting clear expectations, and accountability are a few ways Sam has learned to take charge of all aspects of his life, and the practice of journaling has helped him do it.

> When you take charge of your life, there is no longer need to ask permission of other people or society at large. When you ask permission, you give someone veto power over your life.
>
> Abert F. Geoffrey

JOURNAL YOUR PROGRESS

Logging your progress can also be an effective way to stay motivated when it comes to exercising. A daily exercise program is something everyone should be taking charge of on an ongoing basis. It is a primary and foundational key to health, longevity, and sustained energy. You can tap into this unlimited energy source by exercising at least forty-five minutes six days a week. Have some sort of activity, such as walking the dog, playing tennis, or mowing the lawn, that you do forty-five minutes every day. Then log it in your journal.

Another thing you can log is your sleep patterns. Getting eight hours of sleep each night on an ongoing basis is a small thing you can take charge of to gain enormous payoffs. You need to rest and recover to grow. While we're on the subject, you also need to hydrate. Drinking eight glasses of water every day is a small thing you can take charge of that will transform your health. Sometimes taking charge of the relatively small things can make the biggest difference. Eat clean, exercise every day, get adequate rest every night, and properly hydrate. Taking charge of those fundamentals will do amazing things for your health and fitness. And isn't that really why you're reading this book?

If you're not already exercising on a daily basis, start small. Just get out there and walk for thirty minutes and intentionally begin building your strength and stamina by working on a simple exercise program you can do at home. If it's impractical for you to join a gym, I suggest investing in some inexpensive hand weights. For now, if you don't have hand weights or dumbbells at home, start with milk jugs.

Don't underestimate yourself. You will be surprised how quickly you get stronger. Be prepared to increase your weight after only a couple of weeks.

And remember: You can do anything five more times.

> How am I going to live today to create the tomorrow I'm committed to?
>
> Anthony Robbins

Until one is committed,

there is hesitancy,

the chance to draw back,

always ineffectiveness.

Concerning all acts of initiative (and creation),

there is one elementary truth,

the ignorance of which kills countless ideas and splendid plans:
the moment one definitely commits oneself,
then providence moves too. . . .

W. H. Murray

Listen to yourself.

Learn from yourself.

Allow yourself to grow and to change.

Most of all, allow yourself . . . to believe in YOU.

HARNESS THE POWER OF HUMILITY, HONESTY, AND HUMOR

CHAPTER 12

> A sense of humor is the ability to understand a joke—and that the joke is oneself.
>
> Clifton Paul Fadiman

We've come to the final action step in developing motivational STRENGTH. You've set SMART goals, thought about what you want, revved up your relationships, empowered yourself, negated the negatives, given back with gratitude, and started taking charge of your life. You've seen what to do when the going gets tough, but what about when the going gets good, when you've got it going on and the only thing getting stronger is your sense of pride? To keep your motivation strong, to keep that creative tension from dissipating, you need to learn to *harness the power of humility, honesty, and humor.*

Let's start with humility. It's not something we generally consider a positive thing, but a humbling experience is something we all need. Oddly enough, amazing strength comes from being humbled. When we come face-to-face with our shortcomings and are forced to be honest with ourselves, we begin to grow.

The other day I was having lunch with two friends I hadn't seen in a while. Both were doing great and had achieved some amazing things. One had recently tested for state boards in sociology but was surprised to discover she had failed the math portion. She said reflectively, "Boy, was that humbling."

I thought for a moment how I had been humbled in the past few months and realized that being grounded now and again is very good for the soul. It doesn't mean you have to get down on yourself, but it does mean you have to come down off your pedestal—hopefully before you get knocked off.

Sometimes when we're at the top of our game, we forget to pay attention to our attitude. To stay sharp, we've got to stay humble. Confidence is a beautiful thing, but overconfidence is not. The inner strength that got us where we are, those innate gifts and talents buoyed by a healthy self-assurance, can easily cause us to become complacent if we're not careful.

When we're faced with a new challenge, the tension created keeps us alert to our own weaknesses, and this mindfulness causes us to grow and get stronger. But the tension dissipates once the challenge of what we're doing fades away, and so does our level of self-awareness.

You see this happen a lot in Hollywood, where a formerly struggling actress suddenly becomes a demanding diva, or in the workplace when a once-friendly coworker gets promoted and now you can't even communicate with him or her anymore. For better or for worse, those are the people who will never fulfill their true potential. They stop growing as soon as they believe they've arrived. It's pretty shortsighted, if you think about it.

I like what football legend Frank Leahy said: "Egotism is the anesthetic that dulls the pain of stupidity." If you believe you've "made it" and that's all there is, you are selling yourself short. If indeed you truly think you've "arrived," then that's the time you should start thinking about how to help others reach their destinations. When you do, you'll discover you're only at the beginning of the most important journey of your life.

> With courage you will dare to take risks, have the strength to be compassionate, and the wisdom to be humble.
>
> Keshavan Nair

BE HONEST ABOUT HUMBLE BEGINNINGS

It's a good thing to remember how far you've come. Always be honest with yourself about where you started out and how you got to be where you are. You didn't arrive there alone. If it weren't for others being willing to encourage and coach you, certainly you would not have achieved all you have.

Old-time preacher Ralph W. Sockman once said, "True humility is intelligent self-respect which keeps us from thinking too highly or too meanly of ourselves. It makes us modest by reminding us how far we have come short of what we can be." It's one thing to be humbled by how far you've come and another to be humbled by how far you have yet to go.

The wondrous thing about life is that you never, ever become all you could possibly be. There is always more. No matter what you manage to accomplish, you never really fully maximize your potential. In a sense, your potential is limitless, and being honest about that is truly humbling.

One evening, my good friend Allegra and I met for a glass of wine. As we were catching up, filling in the gaps of the past year and talking about our goals and plans, she asked a profound question: "Are you guided by ego or by confidence and courage?" She went on to differentiate these two concepts by explaining that the ego will essentially keep you the big fish in a little pond, while confidence and real courage will allow you to take risks, to start over if necessary as the little fish in a big pond. Was I willing to give a real go at greatness? Shortly after this conversation, I allowed my confidence and courage to put my ego to rest.

Honesty, humility, and humor will keep the ego from overinflating. Be honest with yourself about where you've come from and how far you have yet to go, be humble as you develop the assets you've been given, and, above all else, never lose your sense of humor. This will keep you from the pit of pride.

Once you have fallen victim to a prideful nature, you'll never be able to appreciate the value of what you have to build on your gifts. Yes, *gifts*. Never forget that your talents and skills and opportunities are gifts. Be grateful. If you don't esteem and appreciate what you have been given, it will fall away. At the very least, you'll lose the *joy* of having it. And without humility, you will lack the capacity to be grateful.

"Pride slays thanksgiving," wrote Henry Ward Beecher, "but a humble mind is the soil out of which thanks naturally grow." He added, "A proud man is seldom a grateful man, for he never thinks he gets as much as he deserves." I have fallen into this trap on more than one occasion. I have thought I deserved more when I should have been grateful for what I had. I've taken my position for granted, and what was granted was taken away.

I've learned the hard lesson of haughtiness, and as a result I don't hesitate to remind myself of my humble beginnings. The fact that I am nothing special is what makes me special, and it's why I'm convinced *everyone* is special. I started out as a typical rebellious teenager and disappointed more people than I care to count. It was only because of some great opportunities I chose to take advantage of, and because I considered both my strengths *and* my weaknesses, that I grew. Often my weaknesses got the better of me and I had to come to the end of my own rope, where I could either hang myself or make a knot and climb back up. Thankfully, by the grace of God, I was always able to climb back up. But I can't forget the fact that I've dangled from the end of some pretty long ropes.

There was a period of time that I poignantly and painfully remember when I did forget my humbling days. When I was a bit younger, I trained a popular news anchor in Chicago and thought I was untouchable. I was doing a lot of television work, some ads and weekly news spots, and was pretty proud of myself. A situation arose that I handled very inappropriately, and the rug was jerked right out from under me.

I was scheduled to do a training session when another trainer walked in and took over. I had no idea who this person was, so I got pretty annoyed and said, "What's going on here? Nobody asked me." I don't know what I was thinking. It turned out that this trainer had her own line of workout videos. I completely offended her and made a complete fool of myself in the process. My training arrangement abruptly ended right there.

I learned a lot from that experience. Now when I work with people in the media, or anyone for that matter, I've learned to keep myself in check. I don't act like I am better than anybody . . . *ever*. At that time, I had been given so much so quickly that I had gotten a little full of myself. I thought I was so cool. I really watch out for this attitude now, and when I coach others, especially trainers and people in the spotlight, I remind them to not fall prey to pride and make the same mistake I did.

As you're moving forward, always remember that when the going gets really good, you need to take a step back and humble yourself—because if you don't, someone or something else will.

> Humility is the only true wisdom by which we prepare our minds for all the possible changes of life.
>
> George Arliss

I CAN LAUGH NOW

Being able to laugh at yourself is essential to staying humble. Now I can look back at my arrogance and what happened as a result, and I can chuckle. I think having a sense of humor—being able to laugh at yourself and not taking yourself too seriously—is what keeps a person grounded. Be grateful for everything you have to offer, be honest about what you don't, and then allow yourself to make mistakes. Take responsibility for your actions and apologize when necessary. That's humility. Being able to humbly say, "Thank you for putting up with me," and "Forgive me; I was wrong," are two things most people are never able to do. "Nobody stands taller than those willing to stand corrected," said the famed *New York Times* columnist William Safire.

There's nothing like a healthy sense of humor to sweeten the medicine of admitting your faults and receiving correction. "Self-deprecating humor can be a healthy reminder that we are not the center of the universe, that humility is our proper posture before our fellow humans as well as before almighty God," wrote Dr. Terry Lindvall, author of *Surprised by Laughter: The Comic World of C.S. Lewis.* He quotes C.S. Lewis as saying, "I suppose we should mind humiliation less if we were but humbler."

> Laughter is a divine gift to the human who is humble. A proud man cannot laugh because he must watch his dignity; he cannot give himself over to the rocking and rolling of his belly. But a poor and happy man laughs heartily because he gives no serious attention to his ego. . . . Only the truly humble belong to this kingdom of divine laughter. . . . Humor and humility should keep good company.[54]

Humor and humility do make good companions. Both are definitely stress relievers. Even more so, humor has a healing effect I'm sure you've read about before. We've all heard the old proverb, "A merry heart does good, like medicine."[55] What is it about being merry that makes for such good medicine? "For decades, researchers have explored how humor helps patients relieve stress and heal," according to *ScienceDaily*. As a result of her study, Dr. Melissa B. Wanzer at Canisius College in Buffalo, New York, found that people "who used humor more frequently reported greater coping efficacy, which led to greater life satisfaction."[56]

Texas A&M psychologist David H. Rosen took his findings one step further and concluded that because humor relieves stress and enhances feelings of well-being, it feeds our sense of hope: "Humor may competitively inhibit negative thoughts with positive ones, and in so doing, foster hope in people. . . . Such a process, Rosen says, could lead to a person experiencing a greater sense of self-worth when dealing with specific problems or stressful events." As a result, "positive emotions could, in turn, lead to an increase in a person's ability to develop a 'plan of attack' for a specific problem as well as increase a person's perceived ability to overcome obstacles in dealing with that problem."[57] These two aspects are specifically what psychologists believe create a sense of hopefulness.

Humor is an emotional mechanism that physiologically deactivates negative thinking. Civil War abolitionist Thomas Higginson wrote, "There is no defense against

---

54. This and the preceding quotation are from C.S. Lewis as quoted by Terry Lindvall, *Surprised by Laughter* (Nashville, TN: Thomas Nelson, 1996), 131.

55. *The New King James Version* (Nashville: Thomas Nelson, 1996), Proverbs 17:22.

56. This and the preceding quotation are from "Laughter Is the Best Medicine," *ScienceDaily*, January 26, 2008, http://www.sciencedaily.com/releases/2008/01/080124200913.htm (accessed May 1, 2009).

57. This and the preceding two quotations are from Texas A&M University, "Humor Can Increase Hope, Research Shows," *ScienceDaily*, April 13, 2005, http://www.sciencedaily.com/releases/2005/04/050413091232.htm (accessed May 15, 2009).

adverse fortune which is so effectual as an habitual sense of humor."

Humor is what keeps us grounded and balanced. It's what enables us to cope and hope in the future and continue believing for the best. It's what causes us to continue bouncing back time after time. It keeps us honest, humble, and sane. "A sense of humor is needed armor," wrote journalist Hugh Sidey. "Joy in one's heart and some laughter on one's lips are signs that the person down deep has a pretty good grasp of life."

> A person without a sense of humor is like a wagon without springs. It's jolted by every pebble on the road.
>
> Henry Ward Beecher

MOTIV8N' SAM

There are some components of humility I really find fascinating. The first one is the ability to laugh at yourself, to not take yourself quite so seriously, and to take it down a notch every now and then. Like gratitude, this is something many of us need to work on daily. Sam does as well. He can laugh at himself, but it took some time to get him to realize what about himself he really found funny, intriguing even.

Another component of humility I find fascinating is how it grows while helping others. When you're humble enough to put someone else's needs before your own, you quickly realize the many things you have taken for granted.

I have seen this in Sam. He's made some wonderful developments in patience and his ability to deal with people in what would have been difficult situations for him before. I have begun to see the deep love and care he shows for the people around him and for the people who need him. He has started to let his loyalty shine and has opened and softened his heart a bit to nurture his relationships and find opportunities to volunteer.

Humility, honesty, and humor can be tough to develop, but they will create the strength of character to help you face any challenge.

> You can turn painful situations around through laughter.
>
> Bill Cosby

IT TAKES CHARACTER TO BE A CHARACTER

Humor and honesty both require humility. Humility is the core component determining a person's strength of character, which is critical to motivational STRENGTH. Without a healthy dose of humility, we will most certainly lack the capacity to be honest with ourselves. Humility makes it all work: it's the oil in the machinery of our character.

Humor facilitates honesty and humility. Sometimes we need a dose of humor to allow us to come to terms with reality. "Humor is something that thrives between man's aspirations and his limitations," said comedian Victor Borge. "There is more logic in humor than in anything else. Because, you see, humor is truth." Humor, that "something that thrives between your aspirations and your limitations" is a transparency of reality, of truth.

Honest self-evaluation can often prove to be rather humorous. It brings you face-to-face with your true self. I love this quote attributed to Francis Bacon: "Imagination was given to man to compensate him for what he is not; a sense of humor to console him for what he is." The capacity to imagine, accompanied by a stabilizing sense of humor, is what makes a great leader. Emotional intelligence and leadership consultant Bruna Martinuzzi suggests that humble leaders are by no means timid but instead are extraordinary visionaries who simply keep an honest view of themselves. Martinuzzi explains, "We often confuse humility with timidity. . . . Humility is all about maintaining our pride about who we are, about our achievements, about our worth—but without arrogance." She adds that essentially it's all about "a quiet confidence. . . . It's about being content to let others discover the layers of our talents without having to boast about them. It's a lack of arrogance, not a lack of aggressiveness in the pursuit of achievement."

Martinuzzi writes that humility "opens us up to possibilities, as we choose open-mindedness and curiosity over protecting our point of view. We spend more time in that wonderful space of the beginner's mind, willing to learn from what others have to offer. We move away from pushing into allowing, from insecure to secure, from seeking approval to seeking enlightenment. We forget about being perfect and we enjoy being in the moment.[58]

Learning to be "in the moment" is humbling, honest, and humorous. It will require you to be transparent, to function from your authentic self, and to laugh at yourself. Yet at the same time, "Humility leads to strength and not to weakness," writes presidential advisor John McCloy. "It is the highest form of self-respect to admit mistakes and to make amends for them."

Most of us spend our adult lives making amends for our mistakes. The most effective way we can do that is by teaching others how to avoid making the mistakes we've made. This is how we leave our greatest legacy. And remember that part of being a good role model and leader is being transparent, living beyond the limitations of some façade by being outward-focused rather than inward-focused. If you don't offer your lessons of humility, not only do you suffer, but so do all those whom you could have reached out to if you hadn't been so self-absorbed.

> Many people believe that humility is the opposite of pride, when, in fact, it is a point of equilibrium. The opposite of pride is actually a lack of self-esteem. A humble person is totally different from a person who cannot recognize and appreciate himself as part of this world's marvels.
>
> Rabino Nilton Bonder

When I think of a great leader, I think of one who has risen to the top of his needs

---

58. This and the preceding two quotations are from Bruna Martinuzzi, "Humility: The Most Beautiful Word in the English Language," *MindTools*, 2006-2007, http://www.mindtools.com/pages/article/newLDR_69.htm (accessed May 15, 2009).

hierarchy and as a result is less preoccupied with himself than with the needs of the rest of the world. To quote management expert Ken Blanchard, "Humility does not mean you think less of yourself. It means you think of yourself less." Blanchard, among others, advocates the importance of what has come to be called "servant leadership" in creating lasting positive change. Rather than being served, servant leaders are stewards who are actively engaged in the service of the greater good. When I think of someone who is self-actualized, I think of a person who is more focused on stewarding one's strength than on showing it off. When you see your assets as something you should be stewarding instead of storing, whether money, abilities, or knowledge, you will continue to grow stronger. The less you think of yourself, the more effective you will become.

The more you are motivated by the needs of others, the more motivated you will be. This is what I call motivational maturity. It's when your strength is fueled by what you can do for other people rather than what they can do for you. That's why I always say, "What motivates me is motivating you." That's really the philosophy behind *Motiv8n' U*.

It's you grabbing hold of these concepts and then embracing the explosive power of motivating others. Nothing will sustain your motivational STRENGTH more than getting fired up about motivating the people around you.

Leo Buscaglia, best-selling author and pioneering speaker on the power of love, once said, "Too often we underestimate the power of a touch, a smile, a kind word, a listening ear, an honest accomplishment, or the smallest act of caring, all of which have the potential to turn a life around." He argued that social connectedness is essential to personal motivation and "transcending the stresses of everyday life." When you are able to look at those around you and say with excitement, "Motivating you motivates me," you will have developed the motivational maturity and strength of a champion. You'll have tapped into an endless source of energy and motivation.

One of my favorite quotes is from Pulitzer Prize-winning author Eudora Welty: "My continuing passion is to part a curtain, that invisible shadow that falls between people, the veil of indifference to each other's presence, each other's wonder, each other's human plight." Harnessing the power of humility, honesty, and humor means living less for yourself than for others. It means taking your eyes off of yourself and looking into the life of someone else. It's about getting up in the morning and gathering strength to offer that strength to someone who needs it.

What motivates me most is motivating you to motivate someone else to motivate someone else! It creates an exponential chain reaction. If I can motivate you to motivate eight people who will each motivate eight people to motivate eight more people, think how quickly your whole community, city, state, nation—the entire world—will get motivated to motivate someone!

We should all be grateful for every breath we take and every new day we have, to not just live but to give. Remembering we're only on this planet for a brief time and that everyone is made of flesh and blood will help you keep things in perspective and keep your priorities straight. Being mindful of your mortality will keep you humble and motivate you to make the most of each day. How would you live today knowing it might be your last? How would you treat someone if you knew it was his or her last day to live?

I recently read a story that made me stop and think about the uncertainty and brevity of life and the power we each have to leave a legacy. One line really captured my attention: "Her humility strengthened her resolve to rise above who she had once been."[59] That powerful statement alone was enough to give me pause, but then I read on:

> Jacqui was grateful. She saw that she'd been given a precious gift, and that no matter what future lay before her, she would never take it for granted. So, when she was diagnosed with non-Hodgkin's Lymphoma and was progressively given news that her body was failing her, her sense of humility and gratitude never left her. In the latter stages of her sickness when all physical hope was lost, she wrote a friend a letter in which she referenced a passage of Scripture that had encouraged her deeply:

> We have this treasure in jars of clay to show that this all-surpassing power is from God and not from us. We are hard pressed on every side, but not crushed; perplexed, but not in despair; persecuted, but not abandoned; struck down, but not destroyed. . . . All this is for your

59. John Michalak, "Humility and Gratitude," *Life Is Relationship*, June 2007, http://www.johnmichalak.com/2009/05/humility-and-gratitude/ (accessed May 15, 2009).

benefit, so that the grace that is reaching more and more people may cause thanksgiving to overflow to the glory of God. Therefore we do not lose heart. Though outwardly we are wasting away, yet inwardly we are being renewed day by day. For our light and momentary troubles are achieving for us an eternal glory that far outweighs them all. So we fix our eyes not on what is seen, but on what is unseen. For what is seen is temporary, but what is unseen is eternal.[60]

I think of the "temporary" and "seen" things of this world as being the extrinsic motivators that don't provide the motivational STRENGTH you need to leave the mark you are capable of leaving. The "eternal" and "unseen" things are those intrinsic motivators that can only be felt within the heart. The more you operate from a place of humility, honesty, and humor, the more you strengthen your connection to the unseen and eternal motivational force you carry within.

Helen Keller once said, "The best and most beautiful things in this world cannot be seen or even heard, but must be felt with the heart." The motivational STRENGTH you carry in your heart is the beautiful thing you have to share with others. When you do, you *will* change the world.

Jacqui's story ended with a lesson we can all learn from. The author wrote: "Freed from her own self-indulgence, Jacqui was able to see that (1) we should be humbled by the fact that none of us are guaranteed our next breath, and that (2) we should be grateful for the life we have been given."[61] With those two things in mind, how will you choose to live the life you've been given?

> Humility does not mean thinking less of yourself than of other people, nor does it mean having a low opinion of your own gifts. It means freedom from thinking about yourself at all.
>
> William Temple

60. John Michalak, "Humility and Gratitude," *Life Is Relationship*, June 2007, http://www.johnmichalak.com/2009/05/humility-and-gratitude/ (accessed May 15, 2009); *The New King James Version* (Nashville: Thomas Nelson, 1996), 2 Corinthians 4:7-9, 15-18.

61. John Michalak, "Humility and Gratitude," *Life Is Relationship*, June 2007, http://www.johnmichalak.com/2009/05/humility-and-gratitude/ (accessed May 15, 2009).

THE HEART OF THE MATTER

It's really a heart issue. Being honest and humble and having a sense of humor will give you the confidence you need to never lose hope. All of these things take place in your heart. Feed your heart; guard your heart; do whatever you do with all of your heart. Remembering that all of us make crazy mistakes, and despite our best intentions will continue to make them, will keep you laughing.

My good friend Alicia exemplifies humility and honesty and the extraordinary power of humor. She is the perfect example of beauty inside and out—incredibly smart, creative, entrepreneurial, and amazingly fit. She has kept me humble for ten years and taught me most of what I know about humility. Lish is the kind of friend who will always be there. She's the friend I can pick up with where I left off, never having to feel defensive about how life got in the way. She is the one person who has seen me at my worst, already knows all of the bad, and has helped me over the course of a decade to find humility and grace to overcome obstacles and weaknesses.

Our relationship has been a nice give and take; we have both been able to add laughter and comic relief to otherwise terrible situations. She is probably the only person in the world with whom I can relive my most painful moments, laugh about them, and still feel positive about my growth, future, and potential. I recruited her to share some of her thoughts about how to maintain a strong core of humility and honesty and a sweet sense of humor, or what I affectionately call *funny bone fitness*.

GUEST EXPERT MOTIV8N' MOMENT
FUNNY BONE FITNESS (HUMILITY, HONESTY, AND HUMOR)

★ What do you do to stay funny bone fit?

1 First, I remember that if God can keep His sense of humor, so can I. Then I think about trying Zumba, or my eyelashes falling off, or how many times I've tripped over my own feet, or the beginning of bathing suit season. While all these things make me chuckle, they also keep me humble.

★ What are the most important things to do every day to exercise humility?

2 Pray daily; acknowledge the wonders of God surrounding you.

3 Listen.

4 Think before speaking. Realize you are not always correct, and evaluate situations through the eyes of both an adult and a child.

5 Take a step back and breathe. Pretentiousness usually stems from one's inability to manage a situation properly. Given the chance to rethink the scenario, would you change your actions?

★ Give some examples of SMART goal prompts for becoming more humble and not losing your sense of humor while doing it.

6 Laugh at yourself at least once a day. Take note of when those times are and rejoice in them. Remember them.

7 Know your life will not be completely fulfilled unless you allow yourself to help someone less fortunate than you. You will be humbled as you realize what you have taken for granted.

8 Surround yourself with people who bring you joy and laughter, and then make sure you return the favor.

Phyllis Diller

HOW'S YOUR FUNNY BONE FITNESS?

What have you been humbled by that you can laugh about now?

_____

_____

_____

_____

List some recent situations where you were forced to exercise your sense of humor.

_____

_____

_____

_____

What role did humility play in the situations above? One proverb says, "Before honor is humility."[62] Perhaps being humbled has strengthened your sense of humor, and perhaps your ability to make light of things has made you a little more honorable. You can use every humbling occasion as a life lesson to become more honorable and to reach out and help someone else.

This is why I love mentoring so much. I am one person who can say, "I've been

---

62. *The New King James Version* (Nashville: Thomas Nelson, 1996), Proverbs 15:33.

there, done that." All the crazy, humbling things I've been through gave me the wisdom and sense of humor to empower me to work with all kinds of people. If I can't keep the rug from being pulled out from under them, at least I know my example will show them they'll be able to stand again no matter what.

I've had the rug pulled out from under me so many times that I've learned how to stand while hopping on one foot! I've also experienced times of lying flat on my back and looking up at the sky. But it was during those times that I was able to see the stars. If it takes being knocked off your feet to see the stars, it's worth it!

I like what Lou Holtz said: "Show me someone who has done something worthwhile and I will show you someone who has overcome adversity." So maybe the most important thing I can tell you is this: Don't fear adversity.

> A hero is an ordinary individual who finds the strength to persevere and endure in spite of overwhelming obstacles.
>
> Christopher Reeve

PAY IT FORWARD

What do you want to have accomplished thirty days from now? Or should we say, "Whose life do you want to have impacted thirty days from now, and how?" I'm not talking about changing people; I'm talking about motivating people.

Best-selling author of *Don't Sweat the Small Stuff*, Kristine Carlson, along with her late husband, Richard Carlson, wrote: "Mental health, loving energy, and good habits are contagious. If there's something in your partner you'd like to see change, take stock of yourself first." After the sudden death of her husband in December 2006, Kristine published *An Hour to Live, An Hour to Love*, based on an extended love letter Richard wrote to her before his unexpected death at the age of forty-five. Thankfully, Richard wrote that letter before it was too late. Don't let another day go by without letting the people in your life know how much you love and appreciate them. Raise the bar and aim to do something amazing on behalf of those you love—something that might have a lasting impact on a host of others you don't even know.

Dr. Benjamin Mays, the late president of Morehouse College, made the following statement:

> The tragedy in life does not lie in not reaching your goal. The tragedy lies in having no goal to reach. It is not a calamity to die with dreams unfulfilled, but it is a calamity not to dream. It is not a disaster to be unable to capture your ideal, but it is a disaster to have no ideal to capture. It is not a disgrace not to reach the stars, but it is a disgrace to have no stars to reach for. Not failure, but low aim, is sin.

Dr. Mays counted Dr. Martin Luther King Jr. among his many students. I can't think of a more humble, hopeful, and motivating personality than Dr. Martin Luther King Jr. Like Dr. Mays, let's leave a legacy of people who motivate people.

WHO WILL YOU MOTIVATE?

I want to leave you with one last motivating challenge.

You can double your motivational STRENGTH to achieve any goal by helping someone else achieve a similar goal. Who will you commit to motivating over the next eight weeks? You can use this as a tool to also motivate yourself to achieve the top eight things you want to see happen over the next eight weeks. If you want to motivate yourself to exercise every day, then find someone you can motivate. If you want to motivate yourself to read a book on financial management, or take a pottery class, or redo your bedroom, then find someone else you can motivate to also do that.

Write down the names of 8 people and what you want to motivate them to achieve:

1 _____

2 _____

3 _____

4 _____

5 _____

6 _____

7 _____

8 _____

CONCLUSION

MOTIV8N' U MOTIV8S ME

I'm so excited that you've committed to taking this journey toward CORE STRENGTH so that you can face any challenge life brings you. Within the last thirty days, you have chosen to make a change, owned where you were, refined your vision and taken responsibility for your dreams, and engaged your whole self in this process toward whole-life fitness.

You've learned to set SMART goals, thought about what you really want, revved up your relationships, empowered yourself, negated the negatives, given back with gratitude, taken charge, and harnessed the power of humility, honesty, and humor.

Along the way, you've learned to balance SMART goals in the eight areas of whole-life fitness: financial, organizational, relational, vocational, emotional, spiritual, nutritional, and "funny bone" fitness. I want you to keep working toward your SMART goals and check your progress every thirty days.

Don't forget to start each day with your push-ups. And keep a daily journal of your progress along the way. Refer back to this book often, especially when you start to experience the bumps of life that inevitably come to all of us, helping us refine our vision and stay humble. Keep your sense of humor through it all, and I know you're going to overcome every obstacle, find true fulfillment, and become everything you are meant to be.

As you focus on becoming fit in every area of your life, remember that you are becoming empowered to help other people find their motivational STRENGTH. Take every opportunity to motivate the people around you. That's the kind of legacy I want for you and for me. The most motivating thing for me ever would be to hear you say with me, "Motivating you motivates me!"

> Do not wait to strike till the iron is hot; but make it hot by striking.
>
> William Butler Yeats

You are stronger than you know, have more potential than you give yourself credit for, and are never, ever alone in your pursuit of greatness. If you believe in yourself half as much as I believe in you, great things are just around the corner.

MOTIV8N' U MOTIV8S ME!

Love,
Staci

ADDENDUM

I decided to do another fitness competition because I was afraid to. It was very difficult and took a lot out of me, but I strive to encourage others to step outside of the comfort zone, and so I did it too. I came in second, which I was very proud of. If you will push yourself beyond the limits of what you think you can do, I know you will achieve your dreams too!

A WORD FROM SAM

When I was asked to do an update for *Motiv8n' U*, I was worried, thinking not much had changed. To be honest, I don't look at the goals Staci and I created that often. After I printed out and reviewed the goals, though, I could clearly see just how far I've come and how far removed I am from the negative lifestyle I was leading.

My *ultimate goal* was originally to lose eighty pounds, which was adjusted to seventy. We thought losing eighty pounds was not a good goal for me due to my tremendous amount of muscle mass and because I wouldn't want to maintain that weight. That being said, I am seventeen pounds from where I'd like my weight to be permanently.

My *financial fitness* is moving along and, although I'm not even close to a comfortable place for me and my family, I am in tune. I now have life insurance (huge stress relief), I have a budget (ever changing, but at least it exists), my wife and I communicate about our finances on a more regular basis, and we have an IRA set up for Amy in a bank we're comfortable with.

Functional fitness. Getting rid of excess is not an issue; we donate it all almost every month. Keeping the right foods in the house has never been an issue, and we will continue to provide whole, natural, organic food for our family as long as we can afford to. I know what is in my fridge (I didn't have a clue before and hated to be in the kitchen because I felt cramped). I feel more at ease in my home, more than I ever have, even though it is my biggest hope/dream/wish/goal to move to an area where I can finally put my roots down and feel secure.

Our *friends and family fitness* is in check, and our family has grown! Amy and the boys have been and always will be my reason for living.

Focused fitness. I am holding on to the dream. I see it, I chase it, and I never lose sight of it. Turning a negative into a positive is most likely one of the best lessons I've learned through Motiv8n' U.

Feeling your fitness also helped me practice turning weakness into strength (pretty hard to do—but when it happens, you feel the win). Tracking my emotions was pretty hard for me, but I do see a direct correlation between tracking and successful weight loss.

Witness the fitness challenged me to volunteer and voice my gratitude. Although I have started to volunteer more, I still would like to make this a larger part of my life and share that time with my family as well. I always felt that it was important to be grateful and to voice it, but as Staci and I both learned, we can never say "thank you" enough!

Feeding your fitness made me take a look at shopping habits, meal preparation, food tracking, and alcohol consumption. Shopping used to be me taking the boys around while Amy filled the cart, and now I take part in it with her. (I think it helps her, and I can be sure to get the items I need.) Meal prep is second nature now, and before it was something that simply did not exist. When I track my food, it really helps keep me in check! Alcohol consumption really didn't seem relevant to me because I didn't feel I drank that much, but when I looked at it from a calories-per-week perspective, I realized how one here or there can really add up. Now I keep that in mind more often.

Funny bone fitness—laughing at myself. I think I have always been able to do this, but this is what it's done: in those moments when I do take myself too seriously, I usually pause and take it down a notch or two.

Motiv8n' U helped me not only with my weight loss but with my overall sense of well-being. I feel like I'm in tune and on track. I may have thought I was before, but standing where I am right now, I can clearly see I was headed down a dead-end street. Thank you, Staci. Thank you, family. Thank you, friends!

APPENDIX

Life Wheel

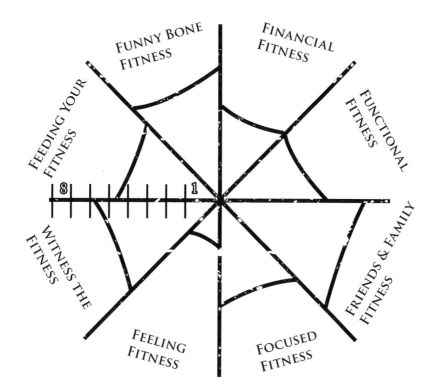

Goal Flowchart

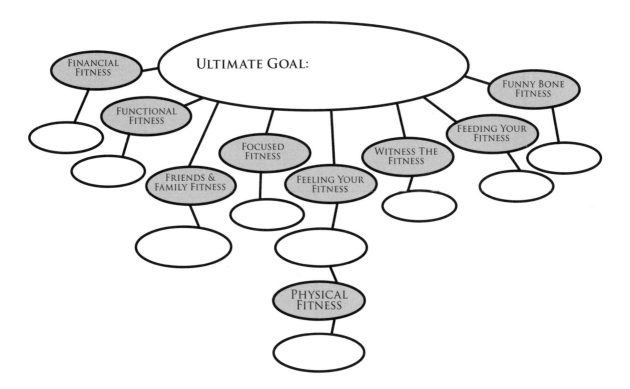

In the blank circle, write down one big long-term goal. This ultimate goal could be anything from losing thirty pounds to finishing a doctorate.

After completing the next two pages, come back to this page and fill in one goal for each area of fitness.

FITNESS GOALS
FILL IN FOUR GOALS FOR EACH AREA OF FITNESS

FINANCIAL	FUNCTIONAL	FRIENDS AND FAMILY	FOCUSED	FEELING	WITNESS THE FITNESS	FEEDING YOUR FITNESS	FUNNY BONE FITNESS

Now list two physical fitness goals:

_____

_____

THIS MONTH'S PLAN

Choose one goal that you wrote down for each life fitness area. These are the goals you will focus on for the next thirty days.

FINANCIAL	FUNCTIONAL	FRIENDS AND FAMILY	FOCUSED	FEELING	WITNESS THE FITNESS	FEEDING YOUR FITNESS	FUNNY BONE FITNESS

Now choose one physical fitness goal:

_____

What happens here is that you are able to focus on the parts of your life that you know you need to address. It may be something simple like cleaning out your closet or calling your mom. But I promise you, the weight that will be lifted off of you will give you that burst of energy you need to work toward your fitness goals. Life is a process. Here is a great way to take charge of it!

STRENGTH IS DEFINED NOT BY THE ABSENCE OF MOMENTS OF WEAKNESS BUT BY YOUR ABILITY TO OVERCOME IN THEM.

My Top 8 Clean Food Picks

Protein

Egg Whites

Chicken

Turkey Burgers

Complex Carbs

Oats

Ezekiel Bread

Veggies

Broccoli

Spinach

Fruit

Any Berry

My suggestion for a clean-eating start: 6 meals

6 protein svgs / 6 veggie svgs / 3 complex-carb svgs /
1-2 fruit svgs per day

Many more clean foods are available. These are just
my favorites!

Top 8 Daily Motiv8n' Action Steps

1 Start your day with push-ups. Set the stage!

2 Have a great breakfast: protein and complex carb.

3 Pack a clean and healthy lunch and snack for the day.

4 Decrease stress by making a to-do list (homework, after-school activities, chores, etc.).

5 Drink plenty of water each day. Not soda or juice.

6 Be accountable for *your* health each day.

7 Get at least seven hours of sleep every night!

8 Take a multivitamin *every* day!

MEDALLION
P R E S S

Want to know what's going on with your favorite author or what new releases are coming from Medallion Press?

Now you can receive breaking news, updates, and more from Medallion Press straight to your cell phone, e-mail, instant messenger, or Facebook!

Sign up now at www.twitter.com/MedallionPress to stay on top of all the happenings in and around Medallion Press.

Be in the know on the latest Medallion Press news by becoming a Medallion Press Insider!

As an Insider you'll receive:

• Our FREE expanded monthly newsletter, giving you more insight into Medallion Press

• Advanced press releases and breaking news

• Greater access to all of your favorite Medallion authors

Joining is easy, just visit our Web site at www.medallionpress.com and click on the Medallion Press Insider tab.

For more information
about other great titles from
Medallion Press, visit
m e d a l l i o n p r e s s . c o m